UNCOMMON SENSE:

A Theory of Human Purpose

Any Commentary or Review greatly appreciated!

JR MILLER

Appendices Graphics by Özgé Genç
Cover Design by JR Miller

PAGE PUBLISHING, INC.
New York, NY

First originally published by Page Publishing, Inc. 2016

ISBN 978-1-68348-141-6 (Paperback)
ISBN 978-1-68348-142-3 (Digital)

Printed in the United States of America

CONTENTS

PREFACE

Socrates once suggested that "the unexamined life is not worth living." Henry David Thoreau seemed to concur when he suggested that "most men lead lives of quiet desperation and go to the grave with a song still in them." Although we may argue that today the unexamined life is common place and that a majority of us are born *already* in our graves, my purpose in this essay is pursuant to the prior perspectives.

It seems reasonable to this writer that most of us would conclude that our lives ought to represent *some* ultimate Good, and that this "Goodness" should be composed (not unlike a song) of a theme or motif in pursuit thereof. It seems equally reasonable that such a quest would logically implicate the question of ultimate human Goodness as the basis for "individual Goodness."

As a self-described "outsider," this writer has considered such motives from an outside-the-box, or perhaps more succinctly, "outside-the-*sphere*" perspective. Therefore, We, i.e., the collective *I's* of this writer, have developed a perspective which We refer to as an "uncommon-sense" perspective. From within such a perspective, one point becomes manifestly apparent—that *everyone* is a (writer).

Everything we think, do, or say is who we are upon the grand stage of human drama where symbolic action *is* the "DNA" of human purpose. From a "commonsense" perspective, it may seem as though reality flows passively and inevitably like a river to the sea and that we are merely swept along in its course. However, from an uncom-mon-sense perspective, quite an opposite view comes into focus—*that we are suspended in a web of symbolically constructed meaning which we ourselves co-create.*

If anything matters, as we assume herein, then every symbol-us-ing individual should critically give and acquire voice in relation to the question of human purpose according to individual perspective as real-time authors within our human drama since what is at stake is much more than public policy, economics, or technology, and nothing less than the ultimate Good of every individual within every social interaction until the end of time.

In as much as we are successful in elevating towards an uncom-mon-sense perspective herein, we should begin acquiring new eyes to see and new ears to hear and to begin critically evaluating meaning while giving voice to our individual perspectives. We should be so compelled not only for the enlightenment of our individual lives, but as a *social obligation* so as to ensure that *no* song goes unsung in our pursuit of human purpose.

INTRODUCTION

If you are human, have a pulse, and are a user of *symbols*, you are inescapably motivated by purpose. Purpose implicates action, which implicates choice, which implicates discrimination, which implicates belief, which implicates cultural orientation, which implicates some modus of rational sense-making rooted in *symbolic representation*. Therefore this essay represents a *critical* exploration of human purpose and its implications in the field of human action through the lens of semiotics based in *Standpoint Theory*.

The various elements of this writing are intended to work together in order to provide an "operating system" with which to examine human action as a function of human purpose and in doing so elucidate the nature of motives implicated within contemporary society.

Although it is desirable to default to the most scholarly of resources in pursuit of human purpose, *this* essay is predominantly based upon the *"boots on the ground"* perspective of *this* writer. However, one such reference is Sandra Harding and Julia T. Wood's *Standpoint Theory*, which suggests that "through strong objectivity and the outsider-within phenomenon, marginalized individuals are placed in a unique position to point to patterns of behavior that those immersed in the dominant group culture are unable to recognize." Although primarily in reference to *feminism* and other traditionally marginalized groups, Harding and Wood's theory is equally applicable to any "marginalized" standpoint. As such, this writer claim's marginalized status as an *outsider-within-theorist*.

From this writer's standpoint, there appears to be particular causality with respect to phenomena which is empirical in nature yet subject to interpretive analysis due to the subjective nature of language. As an aid in understanding causality as it relates to *human action*, we have constructed *Subjective Annihilation Theory* which describes four general phases of action in our quest for the reduction, and ultimate *annihilation* of, subjectivity. Subjective Annihilation Theory, hereinafter SAT, aids us in identifying particular phases of action in our quest for annihilation of subjectivity.

A major assumption of the writing is that human "reality," and thus meaning and purpose, are social constructs mediated through symbolic representation, hence our *semiotic* approach. To expand upon this concept, it is helpful to envision a spider's web as our social "web of meaning." The "spokes" thereof representing our *Axioms* or basic assumptions over which increasingly complex and subjective meanings are spun. To develop our metaphor a bit further, let us imagine a three-dimensional spherical web with the supporting filaments attached between walls of a canyon (representing our connectivity to nature) forming a sort of cocoon of increasingly fine and dense filaments toward the center which represents our contemporary sociological and technological constructions. As we move outward, the filaments of meaning become less and less dense until we arrive at our more elemental attachment points of meaning.

We may thus critically examine individual strands of meaning dialectically on the evolution versus creationism continuum in order to discern "gravities" of Truth relative to our axioms, thereby elucidating the nature of motives in relation to a given filament of meaning.

In addition to our SAT model (Appendices I and II), we introduce our *Pyramid of Power* model (Appendix III), consisting of three general paradigms of Power beginning at the base with the "sexual paradigm," thereupon which rests the "political paradigm," thereupon which rests the "supernatural paradigm." The paradigms of Power are useful in organizing and tracing the evolution of Power within the social structure, thereby elucidating the historical and biological origins of social Power. Locating human action within the Pyramid of Power is effective in analyzing assumptions as to the nature of both natural and socially constructed Power in relation to human purpose.

Our "Hierarchy of Motives" model (Appendix IV) represents a reworking of Maslow's Hierarchy of Needs pyramid. Rather than a hierarchy of more of less passive "needs," we propose an active and dynamic hierarchy of *motives*. Beginning at the base we have motive based in: *biological, control, consubstantiality, ego,* and finally, *potentiality* at its peak.

We use our Hierarchy of Motives as a guide in section II analysis, tracing a general chronology of motives from the more basic at the base of our pyramid to the more ethereal, near its peak.

Finally, we have created our *"Truth, Power, and Good"* pyramid (Appendix V) in order to elucidate the dialectical tension between our will to Power and our will to Good within the field of subjectivity in pursuit of our highest Truths.

Uncommon Sense: A Theory of Human Purpose is intended to act as a sort of gadfly for the purpose of stimulating critical inquiry into primarily exigent social questions thereby promoting a substantial discourse in pursuit of the highest possible Truths. Questions such as: Does *anything* matter? What is our ultimate purpose? If there *is* an ultimate purpose, would knowledge thereof change the course of human action? And if so, in any significant manner and toward what ends?

Axiom 3, "Everything is relative," is inclusive of any statements of fact, therefore it is our intention to avoid making factual assertions. Rather, the entirety of this essay balances upon conditional assumptions such as in the word "if" as in: *if,* and *only if* x, then y. As such, this essay is intended as a dialogical discourse designed to refine "gravities" of "Truth" with which to propose hypotheses of higher "Truth." Therefore, we set about to question any *manifested* "Truths," thereby giving voice to, as well as creating opportunity to give voice to, *all* viewpoints, thereby establishing a dialectic of reasoning from which to analyze the valence of any given "Truth."

Moreover, we assume that *if* anything matters, it is the social obligation of every sentient individual to question *everything* until such a time as there are no longer questions of significance to address. *If* our ultimate human purpose is deemed to be "Good," there could be no evil question in pursuit thereof.

Individuals giving voice to the fact that a thing or condition *appears* a particular way to *them* is not equivalent to asserting a categorical position of fact. However, in a fair and equitable court of public opinion, each individual *should* critically voice his or her opinion according to how things and conditions *appear to themselves*, not only for any potential justification of any given action on behalf of the individual, but for the veracity of all human action in pursuit of human purpose.

SECTION I

Methodology

Subjective Annihilation Theory

Subjective Annihilation *Theory* is based upon the concept of *subjectivity* wherein things and conditions are *subject* to other things and conditions. More specifically, Subjective Annihilation theory, or *SAT,* applies to our rhetorical human-symbolic quest for "un-subjectivity" (a state perhaps more commonly conceptualized as utopia or paradise) wherein we continuously strive to reduce our subjectivity to other things and conditions within our natural and socially constructed worlds.

We have adopted a more primal definition of "subjective" in the title of our theory in order to preserve an uncommon approach to meaning as well as for aesthetics of syntax. The *Merriam-Webster* definition we have adopted is as follows: *Subjective* (adj.) "relating to, or characteristic of one that is a subject especially in lack of freedom of action or in submissiveness." For the sake of argument, it is assumed herein that *everything* is subject in one way or another to other things and conditions inasmuch as *everything's connected* (Axiom 4).

Our SAT model (Appendix I) illustrates four general phases of action within the realm of subjectivity: *acquisition, control, synthesis,* and *potentiality.*

Appendix I provides a top-down perspective of our SAT model which is also a conical representation but herein appears as a two-dimensional disc divided into quadrants of action.

Appendix II provides the conical perspective of our SAT model wherein the cyclical motion indicated in Appendix I is viewed horizontally. The arrow encircling the cone represents either a net increase (upward) or decrease (downward) in *potentiality* or *empowerment*. The vertical arrow indicates the direction toward annihilation of subjectivity at the apex of the cone.

Appendices I & II are analogous to *all* evolutionary processes, however, for our purposes, they apply more specifically to human-symbolic evolution. We first examine SAT as an analog to *inanimate* evolution, then in relation to *biological* (animate) evolution, and finally in relation to *human-symbolic* evolution.

Beginning with the "big bang," the universe has continuously morphed from a singularity into an expanding amalgamation of opposites coalescing out of disparate clouds of hydrogen and helium into increasingly complex forms of matter and energy according to various laws of physics.

As differential pockets of mass coalesce gravitationally, matter and energy congeal to form celestial bodies. This process is analogous to the *acquisition* phase of our SAT model (Appendix I). Once particles become implicated within the matrix of a celestial body, they become subsumed within its gravitational influence or *control*.

Once under the gravitational control of the celestial body, *synthesis* becomes possible as particles combine and recombine to form ever newer particles and elements. Heavier elements differentiate themselves from lighter elements which coalesce or radiate according to laws of physics. The net effect of these processes is *potentiality* (expressed as either a net gain or loss of matter/energy).

What was once a relatively random mass of particles has acquired a net gain in potentiality as a celestial body of greater gravitational influence and a correspondingly higher rate of acquisition. In this manner, potentiality is a function of acquisition, control, and synthesis. Instability in the control phase can negatively impact the synthesis phase corresponding to a net decrease in potentiality. Net potentiality in turn impacts the acquisition phase either positively or negatively as the cycle continues.

Animate creatures likewise acquire energy in the form of organic matter, control matter within their internal organs, and synthesize matter into useable energy through digestion and metabolism, thereby rendering it as a source of energy for continued growth and reproductivity (potentiality).

Appendix I is analogous to all processes within animate nature such as the utilization of physical space wherein animals acquire territory through dominance or by marking it with signs of their presence. By defending (controlling) acquired territories through physical presence and resistance to intruders, they render said territories useful (synthesized) as means to higher ends (potentialities), e.g., food source, procreation, shelter, etc.

Although the cycles of acquisition thru potentiality are analogous to inanimate, animate, and symbolic evolution, the concept of annihilation (which Richard M. Weaver, in his *Ethics of Rhetoric* might refer to as a "God" term) is much less relevant to natural evolution than to *symbolic evolution*.

When we use the term *annihilation* in conjunction with *of subjectivity,* the connotation is that of a highest positive "value" term, hence the God term—Annihilation. If we were to construe the term *subjectivity* as desirable, annihilation in this sense would assume the connotation of a "devil," or negative term, according to Weaver.

From our evolutionary perspective, we assume the universe is neutral with respect to value judgments; therefore, *natural* evolution should neither be motivated, nor predisposed toward, annihilation. From a scientific perspective, the universe appears more likely to eventually "evaporate"—due to the ravages of entropy—and/or be recycled within an endless matrix of multiverses, thereby remaining to one degree or another, subject to other things and conditions.

The God term, "Power," is less applicable to inanimate or animate nature then to human-symbolic evolution (which appears synonymous therewith) since the universe is ostensibly self-contained and therefore cannot spontaneously increase its net Power i.e., potentiality, even if it were somehow motivated towards doing so.

Therefore, the universe, inclusive of its non-symbol using inhabitants, appears to exists in a relative state of *entropic homeostasis*. Should humans achieve annihilation of subjectivity as subordinates *within* the universe, we then would need to reexamine how any part of an ostensible whole can achieve independence (unsubjectivity) therefrom.

Any relationship of a "thing" to *any* other thing *is* subjectivity no matter how distant or remote. Time-space *is* subjectivity. Any word, symbol, thought, or motive *is* subjectivity. Any-*thing*, every-*thing* is subjectivity (with varying "gravities" thereof). We cannot conceive of *absolute* unsubjectivity through language since in order to do so, we must conceive of it in terms of something which it is *not*. A true state of unsubjectivity has no opposites and therefore would not require thought—it would not require!

Subjectivity in *inanimate nature* ostensibly poses no "problem" for itself, e.g., what measure of "distress" do elements suffer as they are drawn into the body of a supermassive star, thereby becoming subject to unimaginable pressures and heat for billions of years, only to be violently expelled into the mind-numbingly cold, indifferent gloom of space?

Animate nature however, is subject to *extinction, death, starvation, malnutrition, physical discomfort, disease, etc.,* and therefore *continuously* seeks to avoid or *reduce* subjectivity thereto. Millions of years of evolution have given rise to ever more complex creatures trough natural selection and successful reproductive strategies, thereby *reducing* subjectivity *to extinction*. As long as a species passes on its genetic code and continues to survive, said species has—in effect—"annihilated" subjectivity to extinction (although remaining subject to other things and conditions such as annihilation due to a collision of its planet with an extraplanetary object or any other cataclysmic catastrophe).

In order to evolve, individuals within a species must not only survive but *successfully reproduce,* this is achieved through: *acquisition, control, synthesis,* and *potentiality*. Plants *acquire* pollen and animals spermatozoon. These fertilizing agents are stored (*controlled*) within the internal reproductive structures of the organisms where the genetic material is *synthesized* into new progeny which represent greater *potentiality* toward continual survival of the species.

Plants *acquire* water, light, and nutrients and *control* said elements within their cellular membranes, *synthesizing* them into useable energy through photosynthesis, thereby rendering said elements available for continued growth and reproductivity (*potentiality*).

An organism becomes more adept in the reduction of subjectivity as it rises in the hierarchy of evolutionary successes. Those lower on the food chain are more subject to other things and conditions. We might argue here that in fact, the lowest forms of life are less susceptible to extinction than the more highly advanced, however, we are referring to the more dominant *within* species as well as the most dominant *of* species, either of which may potentially evolve to achieve *technological* dominance.

Therefore, as long as evolution *allows* for an advancement in the sophistication of a species and technology arises as a result, technology *will* dominate over natural evolution (Axiom 25). Those higher in the food chain are more (potentially) adept at avoiding various subjectivities due to their higher level of sophistication.

Amongst animate creatures, we humans are by far the least subject to our *natural* conditions due to our *symbolic evolution* (a systemic catastrophe not withstanding).

Of greatest significance in our exploration of human action as a function of human purpose is our *human-symbolic evolution* towards *annihilation of subjectivity* and its implications within contemporary and future *social action*. Our examination of inanimate and animate evolution in relation to SAT serves as a conceptual point of departure from which we may view human symbolic evolution as an evolutionary *extension* of natural evolution.

Sometime during the rise of the first purely abstract symbol, our evolution toward annihilation of subjectivity emerged due to our ability to conceptualize *abstractly*. No longer were we constrained to the "here and now," nor the constraints of a sign and its referent, we could now manipulate subjective symbols to *represent* abstract concepts such as that of space-time.

Non symbol-using animals act and react only in the present according to natural laws, therefore they exist in a *relative* state of equilibrium with little vertical advancement in relation to subjectivity (Appendix II), even though evolution itself appears predisposed to a natural progression *towards* tool-using and its implication in the annihilation of subjectivity.

As a species progressively evolves, its upper boundary (Appendix II) slowly advances towards annihilation. However, in the absence of symbolic language, it would be highly improbable that any species would obtain the capacity to become sufficiently aware of its subjectivity so as to *intentionally* reengineer its environment.

In all the universe, there is only one species known to have unlocked the Pandora's box of symbolic evolution, thereby unloosing upon itself a war of words, a flurry of actions, endless controversies, and an exponential rise in the symbolic as we rush *headlong* towards our undefined, and perhaps up until this moment, unacknowledged goal of *unsubjectivity* (Appendix II).

Symbols don't merely enable us to become aware of our subjectivity, they also provide a technology for systematically categorizing things and ideas which can be recalled and recombined into new ideas and technologies. We are able to recall past circumstances and methodologies which were more efficacious, thereby accumulating a *knowledge of technique* (technology) as a weapon against subjectivity.

We are able to reflexively contemplate our natural and social circumstances, and in doing so, proactively pursue strategies and technologies which *reduce* our subjectivity within these environments, thereby rendering them less dangerous, more cooperative, more productive, and thus more *empowering*.

Although contemporary, symbolically constructed reality appears well-rooted in biological motives such as food procurement, shelter, safety, and sex, such natural exigencies have long since been subsumed within the "political"—due to symbolic evolution—as actions governed by master narratives of Good versus evil under the rubric of "supernature," or the *supernatural*.

There are "Good" and "bad" technologies in the *creative* art of living, e.g., tribe A may discover cooperation in hunting as a "Good" technique, while tribe B may discover cooperation in pillaging tribe A as their "Good" technique—where one tribe's "Good" becomes another tribe's "evil." It is ultimately through the Power of persuasion, i.e., through *symbolic representation,* that "knowledge of technique" dominates as Good, or as evil.

Wherein our pre-symbolic ancestors prevailed within the sexual paradigm through physical strength and dominance, we rise in the social hierarchy through symbolic domination (the art of rhetoric), according to Kenneth Burke, by "minimizing pollution and maximizing purification."

As symbol-using animals, we *acquire* knowledge (of technique) which is memorialized (*controlled*) in systems of signs, symbols, and semantics. We *synthesize* new meanings and possibilities of action out of symbolically memorialized technologies, thereby reducing our subjectivity within nature *and* society while ascending within the social hierarchy (*potentiality*). As we continue to reduce our subjectivity to nature (and ourselves), we ascend ever closer to *annihilation of subjectivity* (Appendix II).

Since for us there is no longer any "natural" way of being in the world (Axiom 21) due to the rise of the symbolic, every human act/action is *circumscribed* by symbolic meaning which is governed by political authority and legitimized through supernatural master narratives (Appendix III).

Our symbolically created conscience has made us acutely aware of our ego in relation to culturally specific knowledge of Good and evil. If we are to rise in the social hierarchy, we must either conform as much as possible to dominating master narratives of "Good," or successfully redefine them.

All human energy is thus reducible to symbolic action through which we seek to reduce and eliminate subjectivity through rhetoric and persuasion, thereby rising in the social hierarchy through acquisition, control, synthesis, and the potentiality of technology.

In general, SAT describes processes in both nature and symbolic evolution whereby things evolve from the simple to the complex. In nature, the equivalent of unsubjectivity would be "evaporation" of the known universe, which, according to quantum theory, is plausible.

At this juncture we are less concerned with the fate of the physical universe than the fate of humanity in our search for human purpose since the fate of the physical universe is less significant - in time - than the fate of humanity in our co-construction of "reality."

Whether or not it is actually possible for humans to achieve annihilation of subjectivity remains unknowable since the question is ostensibly beyond the scope of language. On the other hand, there doesn't appear to be *any* evidence to suggest that our will to Power *nor* to Good will at any time, decrease.

If annihilation of subjectivity is in fact the ultimate (latent) motive behind human-symbolic evolution, whether or not it is *actually* achievable is insignificant for our purposes herein since it is impossible to prove within the constraints of symbolic language. The best we can do at this juncture is approximate it as some state of *not* being subject to *anything*, however, we have just described it in in terms of *other* things and conditions—the antithesis of unsubjectivity!

Alternatively, a *conceptual* point of annihilation is *extremely* significant as a rhetorical reference point (as per the big bang theory) in that it allows us to project into the future a theoretical point of unsubjectivity from which we may deconstruct human motives and actions—as a function thereof—to the *present* moment where significance *is* the essence of being.

Since the only time of consequence is the present, it is significant to understand the anatomy of "present" subjectivities in relation to the past and our evolution toward future annihilation, particularly if said subjectivities *are* the motives for everything we think, do, and say, i.e., our co-created social reality.

SAT provides a model for conceptualizing the nature of motives in relation to subjectivity. Whatever "action" is occurring is ultimately motivated by the manifest or latent desire for reduction and elimination of a subjectivity on behalf of its actor.

Every "action" is symbolically encoded as meaningful and therefore significant and of consequence to all symbol users (Axiom 4 and 17). Whether a given action is in the *acquisition, control, synthesis,* or *potentiality* phase, it has the net potential of either empowering or enslaving its actor, other individuals, and/or humanity at large.

The Pyramid of Power

Appendix III represents our hierarchical human *Pyramid of Power* depicting three paradigms of social power. Our utilization of pyramidal models is analogous to universal structures which are organized by ubiquity and simplicity at their bases and merge toward the ethereal and complex at their apexes, e.g., as per technological and biological evolution.

Our SAT models (Appendices I & II) represent phases wherein animals and humans struggle within subjectivity both naturally and symbolically in pursuit of Power or empowerment, while our PoP model (Appendix III) represents both a chronology and hierarchy of human Power divided into three general paradigms, each of which implicate corresponding subjectivities e.g., the sexual paradigm: subjectivity to extinction and discomfort; the political paradigm: subjectivity to inequality, and resistance; the supernatural paradigm: subjectivity to ignorance and prejudice.

Our PoP model represents our evolutionary quest for Power and empowerment arising from the first stirrings of the known universe, evolving toward a theoretical end of time which we refer to as unsubjectivity. It also represents an evolution from the simple to the increasingly complex wherein the apex represents attainment of *Absolute Power*, and thus, annihilation of *all* subjectivity.

The concept of "Power" warrants further elucidation with respect to *human purpose* since anything could be described as some *form* of power. A common dictionary definition of Power is "the ability to do something."

There are metaphysical powers such as the Power of the universe "to be," physical Powers such as, atomic, gravitational, mechanical, etc., and symbolic Powers as in the Power to *control, influence,* and *authorize.* It is these latter forms which we refer to most specifically in relation to the political and supernatural paradigms of Power.

Therefore, our definition of contemporary *human Power* is the control, influence, and authority of humans through symbolic representation.

We refine our definition further by considering three basic forms of Power within our definition: *Power with, Power over,* and *Power apart from.* We define "Power with" as shared Power—whatever "work" is being done is *equally* under the control, influence, and authority of those of whom are implicated and therefore vested in its benefits.

We define "Power over" as the ability to do *otherwise,* where there is a conflict of interest between two or more competing groups or individuals, the group or individual with greatest Power could exercise its will regardless of the will of the other.

We define "Power apart from" as Power which is neither controlled, influenced, nor under the authority of another, nor has control, influence, or authority over another. We use this last definition rhetorically since according to our Axiom 15, "There is no longer any natural (non-symbolic) way of being in the world," and Axiom 2, "Everything is connected." Therefore, there can be no Power "apart from" since everything we do implicates all other symbol (and non-symbol) users to *some* degree. Therefore, Power apart from is a *latent* form of Power over.

The Sexual Paradigm

The sexual paradigm of our PoP model is analogous to the *acquisition* phase of our SAT model, Appendix I, and represents a preponderance of human attributes which were acquired prior to the inception of symbolic language, thus they are the basis of human empowerment in biological evolution.

Such human attributes include the physical, cognitive, and social developments arising as a result of *successful sexual reproduction*. It is less significant who or what survives than who or what is born since nothing survives without first being born. Likewise, who or what is born is less significant than who or what survives *and* successfully passes on its genetic code since successful conception must occur before anything can be born. Thus as humans, our fundamental Power is *physical* power acquired via *successful sexual* reproduction, hence the *sexual paradigm of Power*.

Although successful reproduction is fundamental to *being* born, the sexual paradigm includes all characteristics acquired as a result of evolutionary success, i.e., prowess, cognitive ability, sociability, and reproductive capability.

During our pre-symbolic sexual paradigm of development, it is reasonable to presume that evolution was driven by *natural* exigencies free of *ulterior* motives, and that all behavior was compelled by the interests of the *individual* in relation to its own *Good,* thus the survival of the *individual* is prerequisite to the survival of the species, and the *natural,* primary instinct of humans is *self-preservation*, i.e., acquisition of sustenance and security.

We obtain physical Power through birth which is analogous to a form of latent power *with* our parents' manifest sexual Power, however, our manifest instinct toward self-preservation gives rise to a latent Power *over* orientation with respect to siblings and other members of our species.

Within nature, Power relationships (manifest or latent) are symbiotic and devoid of motive beyond individual survival as opposed to symbolic Power which has the potential of intentionally or unintentionally destroying itself through manifest *and* latent motives of Power over.

Although Power *with,* and *over* relationships are ostensibly in a state of equilibrium within the *whole* of nature, Power *over* predominates with respect to competition and survival of the *fittest* between individuals since empowerment is a function in time (Axiom 29), i.e., the early bird *acquires* the worm thus gaining advantage over "late" birds in the form of greater *potentiality*, i.e., wherever net advantage is being realized by the fittest of organisms *in time,* represents the net hierarchy of Power in nature, expressed as Power of the "fit" *over* the "unfit."

The Political Paradigm

Out of the sexual paradigm emerges our paradigm of symbolic meaning which is analogous to the *control* and *synthesis* phases of our SAT model, wherein meaning is managed and synthesized as potential *purposeful* action.

Rather than a means of efficiently conveying information about what is going on in the external objective world, language *creates* "reality" as we circumscribe and therefore call forth particular *phenomenological* and conceptual articles of significance.

In the pre-symbolic world, there exists no evil, i.e., things are either to be acquired or avoided, e.g., homeostasis is a condition to be *acquired.* However language divides the world symbolically between that which is desirable (Good) and that which is undesirable (evil).

Reward and punishment (Axiom 13) in nature takes on a symbolic *moralized* meaning within such terms as "Good" and "evil," thus relocating the locus of "merit and or guilt" within the *ego* of the socially constructed and hierarchical "self."

Such terms as *life,* and the *pursuit of happiness,* implicate a host of both "Good" and "evil" considerations according to the narratives constructed about them. For example, the "Good" of "life" implicates the *manifest* "Good" of independence, self-defense, self-reliance, and security, which in turn implicate *latent* ("evil") terms such as, defiance, assertiveness, violence, and restriction as necessary actions *in pursuit* of manifest "Good."

"Good," as in "freedom," as a function of "the pursuit of happiness," is explicit in its consideration of freedom to *endeavor* toward happiness which implies the "Good" of liberty, autonomy, sovereignty, etc., yet it also implies servitude, competition, and hierarchy *in the pursuit* thereof.

Where everything is relative (Axiom 3), one man's trash may become another man's treasure. Whatever is deemed more Good or more evil is therefore necessarily dependent upon the consensus of those implicated within a particular discursive community. Every *manifest* "Good" implicates some *latent* "evil," and vice versa (Axioms 5 and 6).

Under the banner of "Good," a particular discursive community may acquire a majority consensus in favor of a particular campaign which is successful in achieving its purpose, e.g., the U.S. Revolutionary War. Such a campaign, although successful in its *manifest* function, may incur some form of deficit as a *latent* function thereof, which, over time, effectively negates the original "Good" of the *manifest* function.

Connections between *manifest* and *latent* functions of "Good" and "evil" are often nebulous to *common* experience because they become significant *over time* (Axiom 29) through the art of *rhetoric*. Most anyone would ostensibly consider taking another human's life as "evil." Yet *manifest* laws restricting such acts, at times, have had the *latent* function of causing others to lose their lives, property, independence, self-defense, self-reliance, and security.

Conversely, the *manifest* "evil" of taking another's life becomes a *manifest* "Good," e.g., capital punishment, in the interest of preserving justice regardless of any latent "evils" which may be implicated therein.

Due to such slipperiness and subjectivity in symbolic meaning, opportunities arise for constructing the "Good" in ways that are beneficial to those in Power, both on the *manifest* "Good" side, as well as on the *latent* evil side, where the *latent* "evil" function is *perceived* as *manifest* "Good" on behalf of its *"beneficiaries."*

Since the inception of symbolic language, all social relationships *are* Power relationships based upon evolving narratives of moral Good versus evil. There is no longer any natural way of being in the world, therefore we *must* conform to *some* bare minimum of socially prescribed behaviors and action routines in order to survive extinction. However, by nature (Axiom 23), we are driven to dominate and therefore to compete symbolically within the political paradigm of *who gets what* in order to rise in its hierarchy.

Power is a function of knowledge as knowledge is a function of reason. Although certain "Truths" can and do obtain *significant* gravities within discursive communities, Truth is *subjective* and contextually conditioned. Our Pyramid of Power model is not necessarily inevitable in its geometry nor its hierarchy, rather it is constantly in flux due to rhetorical competition and resistance.

Within the political paradigm, Truth is a function of Power *over* through symbolic domination. Our will to Power over is not *necessarily* our highest possible manifestation of Truth since symbolic language allows us to conceive of higher Truth based upon Power with. Power *with* is attainable through Individual *voice* towards a common Good resulting in a net balance between our will to Good, and our will to Power. *Who gets what* in the political paradigm is determined by cultural hegemony rooted in ideology, based in values, and regulated by whomever is deemed most "Good" and sustained by the supernatural paradigm of Power.

The Supernatural Paradigm

The supernatural paradigm represents the master narrative of the political paradigm wherein the greatest potentiality of Power is exercised as the ultimate authority governing human action and therefore is analogous to the *potentiality* phase of our SAT model.

There is a force in life which, for lack of a better term, we call "Good." We do not confer such a term to inanimate objects except in relation to *our own lives*. This quality of life, this capital Good, is perhaps more easily elucidated by its opposite—extinction. Dead and inanimate objects are devoid of meaning and purpose and are of no significance *without* life (as *we* know it).

All (known) living organisms have conditions which are favorable to them and therefore Good toward their survival. Conditions such as fertile soil, adequate moisture, sunlight, and temperature constitute the Good in the plant kingdom.

Animals are instinctively cognizant of their Good, i.e., that which to seek and that which to avoid in relation to context. As human nature is essentially animal nature (Axiom 23), we are *essentially* driven by the same Good of nature. This Good is *a priori*, pre-existing symbolic language.

We include quotation marks around symbolic constructions of the "Good" since the Good of nature predates symbolic "Goodness" and is based in natural evolution whereas symbolic "Goodness" is merely a social construction dependent upon subjective cultural values and meaning and therefore represents a compromise with Power over relationships within the political paradigm. However, even the Good of nature has been usurped symbolically as a "Good" beyond the "Good" of nature, as Super-Nature (Axiom: 24), within the supernatural paradigm of Power."

The supernatural paradigm is the domain of the highest *symbolic* construction of "Good" beyond nature. The Good of nature is limited by whatever natural evolution can produce and is subsumed within *subjectivity*. The symbolically constructed "Good" of the supernatural paradigm refines and purifies the Good of nature as *egocentric*, meaningful, and *superior to* the subjectivities of nature.

The supernatural paradigm of Power is dependent upon *symbolic meaning* for its existence and therefore relies upon *master narratives* (stories) intended to elucidate meaning in relation to temporal and metaphysical human exigencies which foster cohesion across diverse discursive communities.

Within the political paradigm, meaning is subjective and contextually dependent. What is Good and what is bad varies between and within discursive communities and contexts where authority is continuously contested. The supernatural paradigm legitimizes secular authority as its highest manifestation of moralized "Good" (God) which exists for the egocentric benefit of *humanity.*

The supernatural paradigm provides *master narratives* which unify contradictory secular and localized narratives (Axiom 11) of "Good" and "evil" thereby promoting cohesion and acquiescence (through mystification) within the political paradigm which sustains it.

A Hierarchy of Motives

Purpose is related to need since a purpose or motive is a response to something which is *lacking*. Abraham Maslow's *Hierarchy of Needs* is therefore most efficacious for tracing the basic needs of the Individual according to a progressive hierarchy. Therefore we have created our *Hierarchy of Motives* (Appendix IV) based upon Maslow's model. However, a few key distinctions are as follows:

Rather than representing a more-or-less objective sequence of minimal states of being which the *individual* achieves autonomously before advancing to the next level, our *Hierarchy of Motives* represents an interactive paradigm of inter-connected *motives* wherein individuals compete within a social-symbolic matrix of meanings.

Hence:

Maslow's *physiological* needs are expanded to *biological* motives which reflect a broader perspective in relation to evolution as the origin of physiological motives.

Safety is placed within the larger circumference of *control,* i.e., a thing must first be controlled before it can be safe.

Maslow's states of "love" and "belonging" are relocated within the *process* of *consubstantiality*, a term proposed by Kenneth Burke which he regards as synonymous with "identification as the key to persuasion." *Consubstantiation* is also synonymous with any communication intended to establish feelings of like-mindedness.

Esteem is placed within the broader concept of the *ego* and its significant implications within the realm of *egoism*.

Finally, *self-actualization* is replaced with *our* concept of *potentiality* (Appendix I).

Whereas Maslow's hierarchy of needs presupposes a self which can be actualized more or less autonomously as though filling a glass with water, our Hierarchy of Motives does not presuppose autonomous selves which can be actualized, but rather socially constructed *individuals* which continuously seek to reduce and eliminate *subjectivity* through *symbolic action*. Therefore, any acquired *potentiality* of the individual is reinvested in the *acquisition* of ever greater resources in the continual pursuit of *unsubjectivity* (Appendix I).

In sum, Maslow's Hierarchy of Needs postulates a more or less autonomous minimalism of progressive requirements through which more or less objective needs are met by the individual as states of being. Whereas our *Hierarchy of Motives* represents a socially constructed paradigm of motives within which individuals compete symbolically as a constant process of *becoming*.

Our Hierarchy of Motives model (Appendix IV) together with our supporting models (Appendices I–V) are all analogous to progression from greater subjectivity at their bases—toward progressively lesser subjectivity toward their peaks beyond which lies unsubjectivity.

Truth, Power, and Good

In our *Truth, Power, and Good* model (Appendix V), we capitalize Truth, Power, and Good, as *God terms*. *Truth* is one of our more slippery of terms, therefore any "Truth" which does not refer to a Truth in nature, i.e., the basic biological motives such as food and sex, we use "quotational emphasis."

We refer to three general species of Goodness:

The Goodness *of nature*: sexual gratification, sustenance, homeostasis. The driving force of all other "Goodness," e.g., symbolic and meta-symbolic. The Goodness of nature is limited by subjectivity in nature.

Symbolic "Goodness": the "Goodness" of *technological Power* over nature/subjectivity. The means to the Goodness of nature through meaningful action, i.e., greater potentiality in the acquisition of the Goodness of nature.

Meta-symbolic "Goodness": the *highest* conceivable "Goodness," i.e., the narratives, myths, & rituals which inform & sustain the organizational structures of symbolic Goodness.

Likewise, we make a distinction between the *Good* of nature, and moralized "Good" with "quotational" emphasis. Since some form of Power or empowerment is the basis of all motives both sacred and profane, we need not "qualify" it. *Power* is understood within the context of its action.

Ostensibly *any* organism would choose to realize its highest Good with the least amount of effort or risk. This is empirically evident among non-symbol-using animals inasmuch as food and sex represent said Goodness.

If an individual were to provide a desirable food source for wild animals, their natural *voraciousness,* i.e., will to the Good of their nature, will cause them to return again and again until they eventually abandon any natural foraging or hunting behaviors in favor of more effortless Goodness.

Likewise, if one were to conduct an experiment wherein a male animal were offered access to two equivalent populations of females, one containing an alpha male and its subordinates, and the other unrestricted and devoid of competing males, it seems reasonable, due to the empirical *sexual voraciousness* of animals, that once the difference was discovered, the subject male would choose the more facile option (Good) as in the food example above.

In our model (Appendix V), point (c) represents a high valence of Good of nature just outside subjectivity (f) of a *hypothetical* organism which obtains its highest Good (e) without need of Power or empowerment. In such a scenario, there is no need for Power (b) since the will to Good which drives the animal is not subject to resistance, i.e., it acquires its highest Good (e), as sustenance, homeostasis, sex, without effort or risk.

An organism fortunate enough to acquire its highest Truth in the Good of nature *without* resistance would have essentially achieved unsubjectivity, since in the *absence of resistance,* there is no limit to the Good. However, there is as yet no known *literal* unsubjectivity, therefore the line between Good (c) and the highest Truth of Good, is depicted as a broken line. Likewise, the line between Power (b) and the highest Truth in Power is broken since there is no need of Power (means) in the absence of the will to the Good of nature (ends).

Since all organisms are subject to other things and conditions (f), they evolve as a symbiotic manifestation of Power and Good (h). They are conceived through the evolutionary Power of their kind and driven by the Good of nature of their kind toward their highest Truth in nature. Animal evolution, as will to Power (as *means*), is perfectly suited to a particular species subjectivity in pursuit of its Good (ends).

With the rise of the symbol-using animal, the Truth, Power, and Good of nature has been subsumed symbolically as *meaningful* since there is no longer any natural way of being in the world (Axiom 21). Although the Good of nature is essentially the same for symbol-using animals (Axiom 23), it has been subsumed as meaningful as well.

What is constructed as "Good" is dependent upon conditions of context and motive. The will to the Good of *nature* ultimately drives human motives, however it has been subsumed within innumerable subspecies of *subjective* "Goodnesses."

The Power of symbolic language is Power *over* nature (Axiom 24) through accumulated knowledge (technology). The Good of nature is more easily acquired through the potentiality (means) of technology, therefore symbol-using humans are not bound to a symbiotic relationship between the will to Power and the will to Good, i.e., more Power equals more potential in acquiring, controlling, and synthesizing the Good of nature.

Within our symbolic hierarchy of meaning, innumerable species of "Good" are subsumed under the highest construction of "Good," i.e., God, which is a superlative, moralized (purified), *supernaturalized* "Good."

As symbol-using humans begin their life's trajectory through subjectivity toward ultimate Truth (h), they encounter a morass of contradictory and overlapping constructions of "Power" as "Good" and "Good" as "Power." Ultimately, all constructions of "Power" and "Good" are subjective and dependent upon who has the greatest Power in *giving voice* thereto.

Symbolic evolution is ultimately a contest over symbols and the Power of naming things (as his-story implies). The highest *construction* of "Good" itself dependent upon *symbols* in order to elucidate meaning, e.g., "I *am* the *Word*."

Within *symbolic* reality, "ends" need not necessarily justify means, i.e., *ends* and *means* are *unlimited* (short of annihilation of subjectivity!). However, means are necessary in acquiring ends. Symbolic *mean*-ing *is* the means to all ends, i.e., *is* Power. Our will to dominate in the "Truth" of meaning is our manifest will to Power over subjectivity (Axiom:1).

The Axioms

The *Axioms* represent a heuristic tool for examining our socially constructed "web of meaning" within which we are suspended. Each Axiom is analogous to a support filament upon which progressively complex and subliminal filaments of meaning are spun, thus providing the foundational assumptions from which to analyze our hypotheses.

Metaphorically, our web of meaning is suspended between the walls of a canyon (representing nature) wherein the supporting filaments (Axioms) are attached. The innermost filaments represent the most recently spun layers of meaning. The closer to the center, the greater the technological complexity, and therefore the more insulated from nature we become.

Although we have attempted to organize the Axioms according to *some* hierarchy of significance, as with any symbolic meaning, the chosen hierarchy is not fixed since (according to Axiom 3) *everything is relative* and dependent upon any given starting point which we choose to circumscribe as "meaningful." Generally however, we attempt to adhere to some hierarchical or chronological ordering in our approach to sense-making.

1. The Will to Power Over is Our Dominant Motive

The concept of "Power" is perhaps one of our more subjective of terms implicating such diverse species as physical, metaphysical, and symbolic Powers.

We propose that *some* form of physical *Power* (means) is the basis of all things as opposed to moral "Goodness." Moral "Goodness" may also be described as a *form* of Power, however, we are advancing the concept that "Goodness," in and of itself does not exist independent of Power and therefore implicates *some* form of Power relationship within the field of subjectivity.

We propose that dominance and survival is the basis of *biological* Power in conjunction with the Good of nature and that *symbolic domination* is the basis of human Power. Symbolic communication enables us to construct our world in any manner we choose, i.e., what one may symbolically construct as a "pet," another may construct as "lunch." Power is implicated wherever anyone has authority in naming things and conditions so as to acquire adherence within a discursive community.

We refer to three types of power as they relate specifically to symbolic Power: *Power with, Power over,* and *Power apart from.* Power with is both a moralistic and utilitarian form of Power, Power over is the ability to do otherwise, while Power apart from is merely a *latent* form of Power over.

When we say "the will to Power *over* is our dominant motive," we do not refer to Power *devoid* of all "Good," but rather that symbolic Power *over* is the *manifest* motive of language regardless of a any latent moral motives Our dominant will to Power *over* is therefore synonymous with Friedrich Nietzsche's *will to power,* and the symbolic "*purification*" of Kenneth Burke.

2. Evolution is the Mechanism of "Creation"

Whether a thing is considered "True" or even more "True" than another depends upon what form of sense-making (knowledge) we employ, e.g., *a priori* or *a posteriori.* That is to say, those things which are commonly experienced (a posteriori), and those things which must be deduced symbolically (a priori).

Non-symbol using organisms posses a sort of posteriori "knowledge." However, for symbol-using humans, knowledge beyond our (pre-symbolic) sexual paradigm has been *symbolically encoded* within our political and supernatural paradigms of Power (Appendix III).

We know how to consume and copulate a posteriori, however, we no longer have any way of knowing in which *manners* (Axiom 21) to engage in such activities *outside* of a priori knowledge, according to cultural dictums encoded within symbolic language, i.e., reason according to dictates of "Good versus evil.".

Historically, a posterior knowledge, or as we refer to herein as "common sense," has dominated over a priori knowledge as a means of sense-making, many such "Truths" seem archaic today, e.g., a flat Earth, a geocentric solar system, the divine right of Kings, etc.

A posteriori, i.e., common sense knowledge, is also analogous to perceiving words as *having* meaning rather than *conveying* meaning, an idea more commensurate with a priori knowledge, i.e, an "uncommon" approach to sense-making as per the *semiotics* of I. A. Richards and the Sapir-Whorf hypothesis. Since words are subjective and *not* fixed in meaning, and Truth has historically been elucidated through the use of words and assumptions based upon a common sense perspective, it makes sense at present to approach the question of "creation" from an a priori perspective.

If we consider the *subjective* nature of language in addition to its manifest evolution toward a priori knowledge, a "common sense" approach to knowledge appears a much less reasonable approach to sense-making. No one can reasonably dispute what another inherently perceives. However, for a symbol-user to attempt to elucidate a posteriori knowledge to another symbol-user, they must *necessarily* digress into an uncommon sense (a priori) knowledge via symbolic (language).

From an uncommon sense (reasoned, scientific) perspective, evidence of evolution as the mechanism of creation is exhaustive inclusive of: archeological and biological evidence, DNA mapping, parallel embryonic developments of the human embryo/fetus with natural evolution, e.g., from single-cell organism, through fish, reptilian, and mammalian phases of the fetus. Additionally, the ostensible evolution of the human brain, e.g., from the primitive (thalamus, hypothalamus, hippocampus) to the addition of the more modern cerebral cortex.

In sum, from an uncommon sense approach to reasoning, *evolution,* as the mechanism of creation, appears the simplest, most reasonable, and logical approach (Axiom 28) toward elucidating human purpose. Although *creationism* presents compelling counter-arguments, such an approach as a *methodology* in sense-making is obtuse and paradoxical, as one must necessarily digress into the symbolically encoded technology of language as its means of Truth-making.

3. Everything is Relative

Many assumptions must be made within symbolic language. For instance, what does the word *everything* consist of? Does it include only those things which are known or are knowable only through language? What is the meaning of *is?* At least one reference source lists three (adjective) quantitative descriptions of the word *relative,* and one familial (noun). We might thus interpret our axiom as "everything" "is" proportional, or "everything" "is" an aunt, uncle, cousin, etc.

Meaning is not self-evident in the statement, everything is relative, rather, it is dependent upon cultural understanding and context. If our Axiom were assumed to be an absolute Truth but written in a foreign language it would yet remain subject to interpretation. Electromagnetic waves are said to have a constant velocity of 186,000 m/s, however, the only way we can achieve such an understanding is *through* subjective (relative) language.

For the purposes of this essay, it is assumed that all symbolic communication is contextually relevant to an individual's cultural viewpoint, vocabulary, life experience, psychological perspective, and a myriad of other variables. However, "gravities" of Truth can and do exist *between* symbol users.

Gravities of Truth are constructed through consubstantiation and consensus within a given context. such gravities can achieve an extraordinary degree of consistency between communicants such as the Truth of gravity itself as a constant force in nature.

Our axiom is analogous to Einstein's theories of special and general relativity in physics, however it has special significance with respect to human psychology, particularly in relation the subjective nature of symbols and meaning through which Einstein's theory was formulated.

4. Everything is Connected

This axiom challenges the assumption that *anything* "exists" outside of language. This is not to assert the impossibility of *any* sort of "thing" existing outside of symbolic language, but rather that the only way we can come to know it is *through* symbolic language. In fact, what do we even mean by the term, *exists?* Is it not merely a subjective term we use to indicate the opposite of things we *perceive* as not existing? And in so doing assert that no other things "exist" beyond *our* ability to name them? And by asserting this, support the ironic conclusion that language itself is the measure of all things?

It may have been of little significance had the universe commenced with one less atom than it actually did *or*—the missing atom may have annihilated the universe (as per the *butterfly effect*) through some imbalance of matter/antimatter, etc. The significance of the above missing atom lies not in the annihilation of the universe per se, but in the way such rhetorical conceptions are possible due to symbolic language.

Although we now know that a single atom has mass and energy and its presence necessarily changes the physical dynamics (however inconceivably small) of its surroundings, the much greater significance of connectivity within the physical universe is in its symbolically encoded meanings *through* which we come to "know" such things and the prodigious manner in which they may be acquired and recalled through symbolic language.

In sum, *anything* "knowable" is connected within our symbolically constructed web of meaning.

5. *There is Opposition in All Things*

Opposites occur ubiquitously in the physical world, e.g., positive and negative, cold and hot, up and down, etc. A pair we refer to frequently within this essay is that of Power and resistance in reference to *symbolic meaning*.

The most fundamental of opposites relative to living organisms is that of *Power* and *resistance*. Life requires Power in the form of energy in order to exist and must continuously acquire energy in order to survive, grow, and evolve. Gravity and inertia are natural forms of resistance, as are competition and scarcity, which all organisms must continuously overcome.

Outside of language, there are no inherent states or conditions of nature, only those which we "circumscribe" (Burke) by giving them names and descriptions. We do this by rhetorically highlighting something as meaningful and distinct apart from its "container" or "background" as in a relief or highlighted text.

We attempt to control nature for our own benefit (Axiom 24) by giving things names, thereby circumscribing them as *meaningful*. That which we deem beneficial (Powerful) is "Good," while that which we deem detrimental (resistance) becomes "evil," *relative* to the needs of the symbol user.

Although we propose there is no *fundamental* Good nor evil in nature (Axiom 6), there are things which are decidedly more beneficial and things which are decidedly more detrimental, e.g., fruits (Good), and snakes (evil).

In the absence of essential Good and evil in nature, any "circumscribed" *manifest* function of "Good" implicates some *latent* function of "evil." Discovering a source of sustenance in the forest (an apple) constitutes a manifest function of "Good." Having consumed said apple constitutes the latent evil of having discovered the resource since it is now no longer available as a future source of Good.

Because there is no essential "Good" nor "evil" in nature (Axiom 6), both manifest and latent functions of one or more symbol users can become multifarious and detrimental *between* them, e.g., the manifest ("Good") function of discovering and eating the apple above could have the latent "evil" function of causing another to starve in an extreme scenario.

In sum, the physical world manifests a continuum of phenomenal variability devoid of "meaning." Meaning is subjective and relative to the standpoint of the symbol user by whom it is imposed. No matter what one symbol user *manifestly* circumscribes as Good *or as* evil, another symbol user may circumscribe as its dialectical *opposite* due to the subjective nature of symbols and differential standpoints. Every manifest beneficial function contains some latent detrimental function, i.e., every manifest "Good" act contains a latent act of "evil." Although common "gravities" of "Good" and "evil" may be established within the context of a discursive community.

6. Nothing is Evil in Nature

According to Socrates, "Man does not do evil, only that which he *perceives* to be good."

In nature, the closest approximation of evil is "harm." Clearly, much harm occurs in nature as evidenced by the existence of thorns, spines, venom, horns, injury, illness, death, etc. There is also evidence of defensive adaptation in the interest of *avoiding* harm such as: aloofness, armored plating, toxicity, etc., yet there is no evidence that non-symbol using organisms knowingly injure *themselves* without some *ulterior* motive.

However, within the paradigm of the symbol-using and *abusing* animal, there exists nearly every shade and nuance of "evil" conceivable. This is because of our Power to name and create symbolic artifacts such as values and morality, mine and yours, yes and no. Such artifacts, however constructed, necessarily serve the best interests of their constructors (see *Egoism*).

If such symbolic constructions are merely relative to whomever's best interest they are servicing and are subjective and therefore subject to *interpretation* (Axioms 1, 3, 5), they are not "evil" constructions but constructions of "Good"—*in service of the best interests of their constructors.*

We propose that it is in fact *impossible* for an individual to commit "evil" on behalf of a purely evil motive. We act always out of our *own best interest* (of Good), e.g., animals do not harm themselves, neither do they commit suicide, nor do *pre-symbolic* infants. All human action *originates* in the will to the Good of nature.

Nearly all sentient organisms can be provoked into a fight or flight response, not as an "evil" retaliation, but as an effort to protect *their own best interests* (of Good). When a human is accused of an "evil" act, most assuredly there was some relatable *perception* of injustice or injustices suffered on behalf of the "evildoer" which precipitated the act *as* justice, i.e., "Good."

Symbolic language creates a method of evaluating—values are *egocentric* and seek empowerment, reward and punishment becomes symbolically encoded (as law) by the empowered and canonized as "moral" within the master narratives of the dominant classes. "Evil", within the paradigm of the symbol-using and abusing animal is therefore a function of *resistance* between competing interests in pursuit of the Good of nature, not a condition within nature.

7. Good and Evil are Synonyms for Reward and Punishment in Nature

As alluded to in Axiom 6 above, reward and punishment are inherent in nature: an organism experiences favorable sensations (reward) in acquiring that which is Good for it, e.g., desirable food sources, sexual conquest, avoidance of discomfort, etc., and undesirable sensations (punishment) as a result of unfavorable conditions.

The entire evolution of organisms revolves upon the concept of benefit versus harm, or reward versus punishment. It is difficult, to conceive of any animal or human performing *any* act without *some* perceived reward (manifest or latent) or desire to avoid punishment. All human action must necessarily *attempt* to conform to the best interests of the individual.

Alternatively, the historical concept of "Good" and "evil" has been rooted in *essences* existing externally to human motive, e.g., one could be *drawn in*, tempted, or corrupted into becoming evil or performing evil acts. The quality of one's soul could be assessed as "Good" or "evil" independent of socially constructed reality.

As such, the moralized reconstructions of reward and punishment as Good and evil perform the rhetorical strategy of authorizing who gets what, who is entitled to what, why, in which proportions, under what conditions, and ensures compliance through supernatural authority.

8. Knowledge is Power

The only Power significant to symbol-using animals is symbolic Power (as per Axiom 14). All other forms of Power become meaningless outside of symbolic reality, but are *constructed* so within. In nature, there is stimulus, response, and memory, but no second-tier subjective meaning.

Symbolic communication allows us to efficiently store and recall past experience in order to compare old ideas with newer ones, thereby improving our technique or *technology*. Knowledge, therefore, is accumulated information regarding technique i.e., a skillful and efficient way of doing or achieving something in pursuit of the *Good*.

Outside of autonomic bodily functions, every aspect of human activity is governed by *knowledge of technique* (Axiom 25). Even autonomic functions depend upon life-sustaining activities which are utterly dependent upon knowledge of technique acquired through *symbolic communication*.

Power is synonymous with communication i.e., the imparting or exchanging of information or news. However, the massive paradigm of "communication" upon which contemporary society is constructed is utterly dependent upon the active (verbal) process we refer to as giving and acquiring "voice" (Axiom 19).

Knowledge is to potential energy as voice is to kinetic energy, i.e., knowledge is the storehouse, and *giving voice*, is the *process,* of empowerment.

9. Power Begets Power

Every advantage in evolution represents a synthesis of those things which are more efficacious toward survival. Due to its subjectivity, nature allows only the successful to survive. Only through survival can the next generation be empowered. Synthesis *is* the process of renewal.

In the symbolic world, knowledge acquired though communication constitutes a record of successes and advantages, however, knowledge is hierarchical (as in natural evolution) and neither shared nor acquired equilaterally. A certain amount of knowledge *cannot* be shared equally due to subjectivity, and another *will not* be shared due to hierarchical competition. Greater technological *means* equals greater acquisition of Goods (*ends,* Axiom 19).

10. Ignorance Is Bliss

Kenneth Burke's conception of *terministic screens* is elucidative here: "Language reflects, selects, and deflects as a way of shaping the symbol systems that allow us to cope with the world."

Language is the gatekeeper for preserving a particular worldview while also serving as a lubricant between members of a discursive community, i.e., humans have an inborn "herd instinct," wherein we instinctively trust the herd as a matter of common survival (Axiom 18).

As symbol users, we are profoundly sensitive to our own judgments and the judgments of others since we seek to maximize reward and minimize punishment (Axioms 7 and 20) within our discursive communities.

The analogy of *Plato's Cave* also serves to elucidate how a commonsense view is propagated and sustained by a particular community within a socially constructed paradigm. Another such analogy is that of the "Emperor's New Clothes" in which the incredulity of the people themselves sustains the hegemony of the status quo, and in doing so, sustains a blissful state of social coherence.

Knowledge is Power in pursuit of Goodness (Purification), ignorance is bliss in avoidance of "evil" (pollution).

11. Belief Equals Reality

From within a socially constructed view of meaning, there is no "reality" outside of language. This is not to suggest that no other conditions "exist" (meaning here also dependent upon "definition"), but rather that we cannot come to know them *as meaningful* outside of symbolic language. The idea, or concept, of reality is merely that, a concept, not a physical inevitability carved in stone which we merely refer to through language. Rather, the *concept* of reality must be approximated *through* subjective language.

What we come to believe as either "True," "false," "Good," or "evil," is based upon values, such as the values of reward versus punishment inherent from our animal ancestry, and post-symbolic subjective values such as whether farming or ranching is the superior profession.

We invent governments in order to regulate human interaction based upon values such as fairness (as opposed to the law of the jungle). We establish religious ideals in order to unify ourselves under common beneficial objectives based upon the value of community over selfishness. Such social constructions evolve from localized interests and represent multiple ways of reconstructing our natural condition.

Although such institutions are artificial inasmuch as they do not occur in nature, they represent some net gravity of localized symbolic "Truths." Similar institutions exist globally yet demonstrate localized uniqueness with respect to fundamental values, thereby exhibiting the subjective nature of language.

Reality is a social construction based upon *belief* satiated by a smorgasbord of values as a result of symbolic intercourse. Wherever one finds oneself acting at any given point in time represents the net confluence of one's beliefs, i.e., one's "reality."

12. We Accept Reality as It is Re-Presented to Us

According to Max Weber, "The last thing a fish notices is the water in which it is suspended." Like fish, we *too* are suspended in the cultural waters of our own making. We are born into a unique matrix of values which preexist us. As infants, we neither understand nor question the nature of inherited "reality."

In *The Truman Show*, Truman Burbank is born as an actor in a popular reality TV show of which he is solely unaware, while being watched by millions as he lives day-to-day fulfilling the lead role. As in the movie, reality is merely an artificial construction which serves the contemporary will of the hegemony.

Similarly, when we are born, we have no choice in the nature of reality as it is presented to us and are immersed, such that we are ignorant that reality is merely a construction in which *we* ourselves are suspended. Hence, reality is transparent to us, nothing could seem more natural and inevitable than the world in which we live.

As we mature and encounter differing cultures and perspectives, we begin to perceive a world less self-centered than that of our youth. This perspective tends to increase with experience over time such that we no longer believe "fanciful" realities of youth, e.g., the Tooth Fairy, Easter Bunny, Santa Clause, etc.

However, according to *Agenda-Setting Theory* (McCoombs and Shaw), those who are empowered to disseminate mass messages hold sway over public opinion not by presenting reality for consumption, but by *re-presenting* (framing) what is "real," i.e., important.

In sum, culture is not something in which we participate, it is *who we are,* i.e., everything we *think, say,* and *do.* Wearing clothes, driving on a particular side of the road, speaking a particular language—all goes largely unnoticed. Although we are somewhat critical of the multiplicity of cultural values presented to us individually, we are much less critical of the *underlying assumptions* upon which they are founded.

13. *We Exist in a World of Form and Substance*

In his *Theory of Forms,* Plato puts forth the idea that forms are more real than the material objects which they represent. In terms of symbolic language, we would concur since we cannot point out objects as significant without common forms for naming things. However, once an object has been brought to our attention through its commonly referenced form, i.e., name or other sign, the substance thereof has *intrinsic* value, as opposed to subjective prescribed value. i.e., "A rose by any other name smells just as sweet."

Plato's *"Allegory of the Cave"* is most a propos in elucidating our distinction, e.g., in the Allegory, the objects which the actors parade across the wall behind the prisoners and in front of the torch represent objects of substance with physical characteristics, presence, and relative value. The shadows of the objects cast on the wall in front of the prisoners represent *signs* of the objects which cast them with no intrinsic value or substance.

Symbolic language is analogous to Plato's shadows inasmuch as it creates images of ideas based in the physical world. Abstract words such as *love* have no physical counterparts substantively but are based upon relationships of physical/substantial beings.

Although we do not subscribe to the *idea* of a physical "reality" outside of symbolic language, nor that language is merely a reflection of reality, language works conversely to the analogy of shadows in a cave by illuminating and highlighting objects themselves rather than merely forming shadows. Whatever is "real" in the physical world is so because we have focused the light of meaning upon such things *through* symbolic language.

Language gives us the tools whereby we are enabled to categorize ideas such as form *and* substance and assign descriptive meanings such as solid, representative, and value. Thus "form" allows us to "realize" value *in* substance.

In the *"Allegory of the Cave,"* the prisoners are easily fooled and confused as to what constitutes true *form* and what constitutes true *substance.* Their difficulty lies in their (commonsense) disadvantaged standpoint, the relativity of reality, and their predisposition to accept reality as it is represented to them (Axioms 1, 3, and 12 respectively).

14. Meaning is Socially Constructed

A commonsense misconception is that words have fixed meaning and merely act as conveyors of meaning, whereas words are arbitrary symbols that have no inherent meaning and are used to *reference* other things and ideas.

If ten individuals were asked to draw a picture of a bird (regardless of artistic ability), it is extremely unlikely that any two depictions would embody remarkably similar characteristics since the word, "bird," *references* a vast array of avian species and characteristics.

If the same subjects were then asked to draw a more specific bird, such as an ostrich, general similarities might then begin to congeal between drawings, yet these too would only constitute *approximations of* an ostrich, not only because of the dissimilarity of conceptual ideas between the artists, but because the drawings themselves *are not* ostriches, only *representations* thereof.

Additionally, words are always contextually dependent, i.e., if one requested the drawing of a bird in a non-English speaking country, one may acquire no depictions whatsoever. Within a kindergarten class, perhaps very abstract renderings, and within a prison, perhaps merely a hand gesture.

Words don't have meaning, *people do*. Words merely convey the meanings people assign them. Meaning arises between persons in conversation as they coordinate ideas around the words they choose within a given context.

15. Language is Subjective

There are words which sound phonetically similar to their referent such as *quack* or *bang*, however, symbols have little to no objective connection to their referents and therefore are *subjective*. As such, symbols are "hollow signifiers," in which meaning is variable and dependent upon context, e.g., the word *gay* no longer depicts a happy state.

Words also contain multiple denotations, connotations, and meanings. If one "runs" for president, is one chasing after a president, or is one engaging in a political contest? If a minister says, "I did it *because* I had a revelation from God," it denotes a somewhat different meaning than if a president says, "I did it *through* the grace of God."

16. Everything is a Sign

That is to say, everything perceivable or knowable is a sign (of something), e.g., a breeze signifies atmosphere, mountains signify tectonic motion, oceans signify water, an animal signifies life.

A road sign signifies the presence of humans, of civilization, of intent to communicate, of technology, of value, etc. Although everything is connected and dynamic, distinctions between forces and phenomena produce signs of their like and kind, e.g., clouds, ocean waves, etc.

Both symbol and non-symbol-using animals interpret signs through their senses. However, humans have symbolically re-encoded all signs as "meaningful." Symbols are also signs, but signs are not symbols for *something else.*

No matter what is occurring in the phenomenal world nor what action a person is engaged in, it is a meaningful sign (of something).

17. No One is an Island

In terms of symbolic communication, any concept of a separate, independent, or autonomous individual is untenable (Axioms 4 and 14). The closest approximation might be someone lost shortly after birth and was raised by wolves.

It is conceivable that an infant could be raised in a lab without symbolic language and survive to adulthood. However, such an "individual" would not be human, as opposed to an animal. Such a being would lack the ability to think abstractly, contemplate the future and the past, and organize ideas and set goals.

Not only is an individual *not* an island independent of the symbolic-discursive community, the symbolic-discursive community *is not* an island independent of the individual. In this manner, *all* symbolic communication is connected and influential over time (as per the butterfly effect). Even an idea or mere thought of an individual of antiquity influences the course of discursive evolution since mere thoughts and ideas are the precursors to behavior and action and all human action is symbolically connected as net reality.

18. There is Strength in Numbers

In nature, greater numbers generally equate to greater advantage, whether in relation to reproduction, intergroup conflict, or overwhelming an adversary. This phenomenon carries over into the symbolic paradigm where a greater number of adherents to a particular *belief* exert potential Power over competing beliefs.

As we have eluded earlier, "gravities of Truth" may be established between individuals according to context. Therefore, strength is a function of the collective consensus of a group as opposed to objective "Truth" discovered externally. An individual *may* have the capacity of pointing out a more coherent "Truth" based upon an uncommon synthesis of existing knowledge, however net strength is a function of symbolic coherence (popular belief) within the dominant discursive community. Ignorance is also a form of coherence (strength) insofar as silence is acquiescence in belief.

19. Voice Equals "Personhood"

Language is by far more significant to human purpose than any given individual. A human lifetime is relatively brief, yet language transcends time and space. Nothing *significant* in human history has been achieved independent of symbolic language. Human animals are born into the symbolic world of language and achieve "personhood" *through* language. There is no I, me, nor individual, outside of language.

"Voice" is the process of sending and acquiring messages, i.e., an *active* voice initiates action, a passive voice perpetuates the status quo. All human activity *is voice*. Every *action* (or lack thereof) and every *intent* gives "voice" to a particular worldview constructed and maintained through symbolic language.

20. We Regulate One Another

All the world's a stage, and we are merely players (Axiom 22), wherein through rhetoric we seek to maximize consubstantiation with those of whom we interact (Axiom 18).

In order for individuals to navigate the complex world of meaning and avoid conflict, we adopt a viewpoint which George Herbert Mead refers to as *the generalized other*. The internalized reactions and behaviors of others serves as a psychological template for how we ourselves should act, and in so doing, we perpetuate behavior modification as we in turn perform for others.

According to Elisabeth Noelle-Neumann's *spiral of silence* theory, when the beliefs of the individual appear out of favor with popular opinion, the individual becomes silent in proportion to the degree of divergence.

21. There is No "Natural" Way of Being in the World

The term *natural* is somewhat slippery since it could as well be argued that if natural evolution is the mechanism of creation (Axiom 2), then *all* ways of being are natural by definition.

More specifically, there is no natural way of being human *outside of symbolic language*. Any human behavior or mannerism prior to the advent of language has long since been subsumed as "meaningful." Bodily functions, instinctive behaviors, and methods of survival, are now conditioned, regulated, and interpreted *symbolically*.

In the strictest sense, there *is* no "outside-of-symbolic-language" nature since language-based technology subdues even nature (Axiom 25). If everything is connected (Axiom 4), then every technological development implicates a ripple effect throughout nature (however minuscule) which forever alters what *was*.

22. All the World's a Stage

Another way of phrasing this is that all the world's a *scene* (as per Kenneth Burke's *dramatistic pentad*), or context of motive. Since there's no natural way of being in the world (Axiom 21), "we" act out improvised narratives symbolically as "we" negotiate meaning, one with another. "We" in reference to the multiplicity of roles which we assume contextually.

All communication is contextually dependent as per the *actus/status* pair (Burke). Any *state* of circumstances is the net results of the acts (actus) implicated therein. The *status* (context) determines which acts are possible, and the *actus* (acts) reifies the status. We are continuously "fixed" within any given scene according to our *acts/status*.

23. Human Nature is Essentially Animal Nature

Other than recombinations of the old, there's essentially nothing new under the sun. Humanity's highest technological achievements are merely biological extensions, e.g., modes of transport as extensions of the legs, computer technology as extension of the brain, and communications technology as extension of signification. All of these complexities and machinations are merely so that we might do *more, better, faster* (thus becoming empowered *over* nature, Axiom 24) than our ancestors.

Every technological advantage essentially serves to augment the *animal functions* of the pre-symbolic, sexual paradigm, i.e., survival, food, sex, safety. As such, all motives can be traced to originating within the subjectivities of the sexual paradigm.

24. We are at War with Nature

This is not to suggest that we are at war *against* nature so as to destroy it, but rather, that we are in a struggle to *control* nature according to *our* will. All higher organisms are *subject* to death, disease, discomfort, hunger, etc. We seek to subdue nature due to our *knowledge* of subjectivity within it.

Symbolic language allows us to subdue nature according to narratives of "Good" versus "evil," e.g., manifest destiny. We celebrate dominance *over* nature through technological advantage and such symbolic rituals as the rodeo and bullfighting.

25. Technology Subsumes Nature

Not only is there no "natural" way of being *human* in the world due to symbolic language (Axiom 21), but technology, as a product of symbolic language (knowledge of technique), absorbs and reconstitutes nature as an expression of dominion.

As technology proliferates, it creates a self-sustaining network of increasing complexity and significance, i.e., the *Dionysian* world reined in by *Apollonian* providence.

The exhausted symbol-using and abusing human *animal* retreats into commonsense reasoning as it becomes subsumed and separated from its natural condition through complex tools of its own making.

26. We're All Vested

All organisms have "special interests" in which they are vested due to evolutionary adaptation in survival. If said interests, e.g., food, sex, shelter were eliminated, they would no longer have means of survival.

We, humans, are vested symbolically across multiple special interest groups, e.g., national, political, economical, racial, ideological, etc. We use symbolic language similar to the manner in which lower species utilize evolutionary advantages in relation to *their* special interests.

Our social "orientation" or standpoint represents our net special interests across all categories in which we have a stake. Each individual's rhetoric is constructed around his or her center of vested interest and serves to defend, protect, and advance said interests.

27. Simplicity Is the Reasonable Route to Truth

This concept is essentially *Occam's razor* which states that in the absence of certainty among competing hypothesis, the one with the fewest assumptions should be selected.

This is not to suggest that simplicity is *necessarily* the route to Truth, but rather that simplicity is more efficacious toward developing *hypothesis* in search of Truth in the absence of knowledge.

28. The Golden Mean Is the Ideal Status

When faced with possible extremes of choice, the middle ground is the most reasonable starting point. Due to symbolic language, *anything* can be pursued in its extremities. If human nature is essentially animal nature (Axiom 23), then homeostasis in mind and body is a higher Truth of nature.

Within the golden mean lies the balance, harmony, and symmetry of nature.

29. Time Waits for No One

If anything matters, that is to say, if there are alternate ways of becoming which might be more advantageous, then *time is always of the essence* in the pursuit thereof.

Anything of significance occurs *in time*, and anything advantageous is more advantageous when discovered earlier, i.e., within subjectivity time *is* potentiality—more time equals more *potentiality.*

Time passes indifferently and unabated. What is possible today may become impossible tomorrow.

30. Nothing Ventured, Nothing Gained

A venture is defined as something bold and risky. As such, it is analogous to the whole of human natural and symbolic evolution. Nothing *significant* would exist in the absence of risk taken on behalf of someone.

No risk equals no reward. Reward is proportional to risk.

31. The Ego is the Motivating Factor in Symbolic Evolution

According to Kenneth Burke, humans have an intrinsic need to rid ourselves of language-caused guilt in order to achieve redemption which is achieved through symbolic rebirth.

Humans wish to rise in the social hierarchy, the highest expression of which is creativity in the pursuit of the Good. It is the object of the ego to align itself with the highest symbols of the Good, and in doing so, perpetuating symbolic evolution.

32. The Creative Faculty Is the Mechanism of Cultural Evolution

As each individual competes creatively within her/his social hierarchy in search of her or his highest expressions of Good, the highest creative expressions gain adherence within discursive communities, and become the intellectual properties thereof.

Since everything is relative (Axiom 3), and meaning is socially constructed (Axiom 14), each discursive community evolves a unique culture.

33. All Roads Lead to Rome

This metaphor encapsulates our idea that *all* human motive leads inevitably toward the *annihilation of subjectivity.*

SECTION II

Analysis

Overview

Our title, *Uncommon Sense: A Theory of Human Purpose,* represents a comparatively postmodern amalgamation of concepts borrowed from Thomas Paine's *Common Sense* and Albert Einstein's *unified field theory.* This essay is analogous to Thomas Paine's *Common Sense* as a methodology in sense-making, as well as a catalyst for deconstructing contemporary hegemony. It is analogous to Einstein's *unified field theory* insofar as human purpose can be reduced to a unifying principle.

If we imagine the concept of "uncommon-sense" as a polar opposite of commonsense on a dialectical scale where *common* is synonymous with taken-for-granted and *uncommon* with a questioning of everything, then what we are promoting herein is a critical questioning of everything. If we literally question *everything* however, we eventually arrive at a reductio ad absurdum (in our *negating of things* through descriptions of that which they are *not*) if our intent is to discover some foundational "Truth," since our reasoning is mediated through *subjective* language which is *contextually* dependent (Axiom 3).

An uncommon-sense orientation to reasoning must therefore arise *from* a commonsense orientation. For example, at some point, we must agree that an abstract symbol such as the letter T represents a corollary relationship with the sound, *tee,* in spoken English, and must conform to rules of grammar as a written character.

To some degree, a commonsense orientation is crucial in acquiring a consensus of meaning at the most basic level. A commonsense orientation toward socially understood *action routines* within such cooperative practices as hunting, gathering, agrarian practices, and rituals is also essential to survival. Thus a commonsense orientation becomes ensconced more as a *grammar* for social cooperation and less as a means of discovery, i.e., a commonsense orientation naturalizes social experience as purposeful, predictable, and structural.

An uncommon-sense orientation must necessarily arise in response to *social complexity* where connections between things and ideas become increasingly nebulous. The symbol, *1*, is *exoteric* as a symbol for delineating quantities of commodities such as the number of cattle, yet becomes *esoteric* in relation to delineating a quantity of meat, where we begin to require additional qualifiers of meaning such as *1 pound*, and even more so as we evolve toward concepts such as quantum mechanics.

An uncommon-sense approach to reason is more analogous to assimilation; to "quantum leaps" of discovery, to epiphanies, than a piecemeal understanding through commonly shared experience. As we rise from a "boots-on-the-ground" commonsense orientation toward a fifty-thousand foot uncommon one, we are more capable of discerning the phenomenal *interconnectedness* of things on a grander scale (Axiom 4).

In considering human purpose from an uncommon-sense perspective, it is necessary to first acquire an understanding of the *anatomy* of purpose with which to deconstruct and analyze its elemental components. Since our subject matter entails meaning with its attendant symbols, our approach is necessarily through the lens of *semiotics*.

In deconstructing the concept of human purpose and examining its elemental components from an uncommon-sense perspective, we have devised *subjective annihilation theory* as both a hypothesis and methodology for examining human purpose. Utilizing *subjective annihilation theory*, hereinafter SAT, as our analytical tool, we have established our coordinates in "purpose," from which we may identify human action as a function thereof. Tracing our trajectory forward in time brings us to a singularity which we call subjective annihilation (an inverted trajectory analogous to unified field theory wherein all forces converge within a singularity).

Section I (methodology), provides theoretical tools with which to engage an in-depth analysis of symbolic action as a function of human purpose. Our organizational approach is that of a chrono-logical accounting beginning with the more primal of concepts pro-gressing toward the increasingly complex.

With the aid of our theoretical models in section I (method-ology), we may "plug in" any node of inquiry relating to human purpose and allow our machinery of reason to aid in approximating "gravities of Truth." Therefore, *no* subject matter is "out of bounds" as long as its aim is elucidating human purpose (although we can think of no topic unrelated since if it can be communicated and has *significance*, then it must needs be relevant).

The topics chosen do not *necessarily* represent the most signifi-cant human motives but rather those which happen to be more con-spicuous relative to *the standpoint of this writer*, at the time of this writing, therefore, any topic (or Axiom) circumscribed as significant necessarily implicates the unique perspective of *this* writer, although we have attempted to select topics which appear fundamentally related to human purpose.

This section utilizes our *Hierarchy of Motives* model (Appendix IV) as a template for examining motive as a function of both natural and symbolic evolution, from the more basic and primal motives near its base, to the more complex and contemporary near its peak.

We begin examining the loci of *biological* motives as analogous to Maslow's *physiological needs,* as located within our *sexual paradigm of power*. Motives associated with *control, consubstantiality,* and *ego* (analogous to Maslow's *safety, love/belonging,* and *esteem needs*) are examined in relation to the *political paradigm*, and motives of *poten-tiality* (analogous to Maslow's *self-actualization needs*) are examined in relation to the *supernatural paradigm*.

Within section III (conclusion), we reevaluate the various loci of motives from a socially symbolic perspective as we consider them hier-archically from the peak of our Hierarchy of Motives toward its base.

If human purpose is significant and the ultimate object of every human action and human action can be influenced in relation to purpose and quality of life is a function of human action, then what could be more *significant* than analyzing contemporary human action as a function of our purpose?

Loci of Motives

Biological (Physiological)

Sustenance

If we consider sustenance as our primary will toward the Goodness of nature, than Maslow's "need" of safety represents a necessary *condition* in pursuit thereof. In this manner safety is merely the subjective medium through which we navigate in pursuit of the motive of sustenance. The motive of sustenance is driven by the will to the Good of nature.

All animals (symbol- and non-symbol-using) exhibit a ravenous appetite. There appears little evidence to suggest that pre-symbolic humans share food equally nor are they morally motivated in doing so. A creator could have created humans so as not to appear evolutionarily equivocal to lower species with a ravenous appetite in pursuit of sustenance, thereby reducing uncertainty with respect to the divine nature of Goodness.

An all-Powerful creator could have created humans so as to operate according to some atomic source of energy or perhaps better yet, according to pure Goodness itself, thus becoming blessed or damned according to an autonomous will toward essential Goodness or evil.

If [man] does not live by bread alone, one may question the case of any pre-symbolic infants which have expired due to malnutrition. One may simply assert it is "God's will" as though it were an apologist's pejorative to know the mind of God in one's application of moral judgement and that God's will must necessarily conform to linguistic constructions of "Good" and "evil."

Thus moral judgment exhibits itself as a product and motive of language rather than that of pre-symbolic evolution. Moral judgement thus becomes a linguistic tool for assigning guilt or praise in relation to pre-symbolic motives in pursuit of who gets what within the political and supernatural paradigms.

The biological motive of sustenance could have been reserved for lower non-symbol using species, however it is implicated everywhere within our contemporary political and supernatural paradigms of Power, i.e., in our quotidian and crass preoccupation with food, and its predominance in both secular and sacred holy-days and rituals.

At the very base of our Pyramid of Power is the motive of sustenance. Whatever else we do in pursuit of Power within the political and supernatural paradigms is built upon continuous sustenance, serves to ensure future sustenance, and ultimately seeks to control all technological machinations implicated therein.

Homeostasis

As organisms arise to fill a niche, there are natural variables (subjectivities) within a given organism's context such as temperature, acidity, available energy, etc. Each organism competes within its domain of subjectivity struggling to maintain a balance of Power and Good in nature (Appendix V).

Once the motive of sustenance becomes satiated, motives of security, health, and comfort become dominant. According to Kenneth Burke, "All living things are critics," which go about discerning between positive and negative stimuli, whether it's avoiding being eaten, seeking shelter from environmental conditions, or attending to bodily functions.

To achieve the highest Truth in the Good of nature (Appendix V) is to acquire sufficient sustenance, achieve successful sexual reproduction, and the most optimal balance between environmental and bodily conditions. The field of subjectivity is the field of unpredictability. Living *is* the process of (critically) negotiating subjectivity in all of its forms and variables in pursuit of *homeostasis*.

Homeostasis as its own reward *is* the *Good* of nature. It is a state within subjectivity which allows a species to arise *and* become dominant. It is the basis for successful reproduction as the highest Truth in nature as a *balance* between the Good and Power of nature (Appendix V).

Each organism acts and reacts according to *individual* experience within subjectivity, therefore, motive is necessarily oriented in the "self," where negative stimuli is avoided and positive stimuli is sought. In nature, Power is manifestly acquired *apart from, as the organism seeks first to satiate its own drives.*

There is a balance across various extremes within symbolic language (Axiom 28). For example, we may suppose that a flying spaghetti monster zapped us into existence for no reason other than she/he/it did. If the warrants given for the flying spaghetti monster scenario are the higher "Truth," then "Truth" is utterly reliant upon this statement alone since there is no other reason available for belief.

Where reason is lacking, any statement may substitute for "Truth." However, one can not rely *solely* upon reason alone in order to arrive at gravities of "Truth." Both animals and humans have a *posteriori* knowledge, e.g., birds know how to fly and human infants know how to swim without need of reason. Therefore "Truth" likewise represents a homeostasis between a priori and a posteriori knowledge.

Homeostasis is a fundamental motive of biological organisms in nature as well as in humans, therefore it is reasonable a priori, that humans likewise evolved from nature. Symbols are meaningless in themselves. Meaningless symbols can be used to imbue subjective meaning as means towards "Truth"-making. Thus homeostasis in sense-making is also a motive within *symbolic interaction*.

Sex

Once physiological homeostasis is achieved, i.e., health and sustenance, the *sex drive* becomes a predominant motive of organisms. The *sexual paradigm of Power* in our PoP (Appendix III) is our basis of Power since although organisms may be born and survive, they become evolutionarily insignificant unless they successfully pass on their genes (i.e., potentiality phase of Appendix I). Other factors also influence successful evolution, however, organisms must *first be born* in order that such factors become significant. No organism arises independent of *successful reproduction*.

All animals *compete* for sexual partners; horns, claws, teeth, stealth, bulk, and aggressiveness all testify ("test" itself etymologically implicated within Power and *human* sexuality) of intense competition for mating rights within species.

Successful sexual reproduction is the prerequisite of human evolution and the basis of Power in species. Whomever is successful in reproduction gives "voice" to his/her genetic dominance in the continuity of evolution. The sexual paradigm of Power in our pyramid model is the broad paradigm upon which all biological Power is based through *dominance,* i.e., it is the evolution *of* Power within the Power of evolution (Axiom 2).

If men were created as moral beings, conception *could* occur spontaneously between couples once they achieved a certain degree of divine platonic love between them and their creator, without competition or gender play. That is unless it is somehow necessary that human reproduction appears equivocal to the biological phases of evolutionary growth and fetal development.

In the ostensible absence of divine intervention and other innumerable manners in which humans might reproduce *outside* of biological analogy, evolution is the most reasonable and simplistic (Axiom 27) gravity of Truth in relation to the motive of human sexual reproduction.

Control (Security)

Regulatory

If one controls a thing, one is not only *not* vulnerable to the thing as a condition of "safety," but the thing itself becomes vulnerable to the agent of control.

Motives of control are not only analogous to Maslow's need of *safety*, but *all* subjectivities. Anything of value which can be organized and *regulated*, i.e., made regular, is potential Power over subjectivity through the process of *acquisition, control, synthesis,* and *potentiality* (Appendix I). The control phase is the primary locus of *action* since one cannot acquire nor synthesize to potentiality except through some agency of control. Acquisition proceeds control in our SAT model since an organism must *first* acquire a body with which to act – a control function of its progenitors.

Within our political paradigm of *who gets what,* all control is mediated though symbolic meaning. Control in nature is a function of the drive toward the Good of nature in balance with Power in nature and regulated within cycles of periodicity, e.g., growth, seasonal, sexual reproductivity, etc.

Our ability to name things symbolically allows us to re-create nature according to our will through accumulated symbolic knowledge. Knowledge allows us to contemplate our subjectivity within nature (Axiom 24) in all of its manifestations, e.g., pain, death, physical discomfort, etc., and symbolically reconstruct (organize/order) nature and society.

Knowledge of technique, i.e., *technology*, is countered by uncertainty within naure as well as our political paradigm. Essentially, technology, represents the symbolic "Good" of humankind, while uncertainty (ignorance), represents the "bad," i.e., "evil," within subjectivity. Technology is analogous to a beam of light which we shine into the abyss of uncertainty, i.e., subjectivity, in search of greater certainty, i.e., Power *over* subjectivity, and a means to even greater Power through the process of *acquisition* through *potentiality* (Appendix I).

According to *uncertainty reduction theory* (Berger and Calabrese), humans are uncomfortable with uncertainty, and therefore seek to reduce uncertainty through communication. According to this theory, uncertainty is essentially "evil," while certainty has a corresponding valence of "Good." In this sense, *all* communication is *uncertainty reduction*. If one contacts another merely to say "I love you," one is merely *reducing uncertainty* with respect to a relational status, otherwise there would be no need for the communication, i.e., if we weren't *subject to* time, distance, subjective/equivocal meanings, changing social climates, etc., status would remain static with no need for reduction of uncertainty.

In order to regulate our subjectivity within nature and interhuman relationships, we must delineate boundaries between that which is deemed "Good" and that which is deemed "evil." In this manner, we reduce uncertainty in relation to various contexts of interaction, i.e., what is prescribed, permissible, or prohibited, according to varying sets of conditions. All actions and interactions within the political and supernatural paradigms are regulated according to symbolic constructions of Good versus evil (Axiom 20) whether implied within the conventions of intercommunication or codified and enforced as law.

Rules

Since everything is relative, reality is a social construction, and symbolic language is subjective (Axiom 3, 14, and 15), contradiction is *inevitable* between and within discursive agents and communities, therefore some system of "standardizing" meaning is necessary in order to control interactions according to some common "Good."

Whenever two or more symbol users compete over resources, some rule or sets of rules *inevitably* arise, i.e., the law of the jungle (in nature). Since language *is* the process of naming things as "Good" or evil, contested "Goods" and "evils" necessarily require qualifying, since we are all potentially vested (Axiom 26) in benefits and harms of said "Goods" and "evils" and since everything is *connected* (Axiom 4).

The necessary "Good" of a rule must be agreed upon by a majority within a discursive community (have a superior gravity of "Truth" in "Goodness"), otherwise, it would have a negative Truth value (Axiom 18). Therefore, any rule in force represents dominance of *voice* (Axiom 19) in the construction of "Good."

Although rules typically arise under the auspice of "Good" intentions, they necessarily do so in response to contention over resources, whether those resources be time, right-of-way, ownership, or control (Axioms 5 and 1).

Although rules are *formalized* manifestations of dominant *voices* within the political and supernatural paradigms, we also regulate one another (Axiom 20) in every formal and informal interaction through the Power of giving and acquiring *voice*. We *give voice* not only through actual speaking or writing, but through status, body language, the clothes we wear, the vehicles we drive, where we live, how we communicate, and the symbols we *circumscribe* as significant, i.e., everything we think, say and do (Axiom 21).

Although much of the time we are unaware of giving voice (Axiom 12), when ideologies and cultures clash, the process of our giving and acquiring voice becomes more evident, e.g., the symbols of Nazi Germany in the 1930s gave Powerful voice to a particular worldview, as per, the Nazi salute. The pressure to conform to such symbols within social contexts is compelling as dissenting voices wither and shrink into obscurity (Axioms 16, 17, 18, 19, and 20).

From a creationist standpoint, "Good" and evil are ostensibly moral states precipitated by the fall of man due to breaking of God's rules. Such a God must have anticipated the corrupt nature of his/her own creation. Evil must have preexisted man since human beings, as divine creations, could not be the cause of conditions beyond that which were imbued by their creator.

An evolutionary origin of rules arising from the law of the jungle is empirical as observed in nature and within the fossil record. Since symbolic language *is* the process of purifying meaning, i.e., the *knowledge of "Good" and "evil,* it is not inconceivable that moral constructions of Good and evil would arise as authoritative rules according to the motive of control. If moral rules are of divine origin, i.e., commandments, they are so necessarily through *symbolic language*.

Rules, as regulatory devices within the political paradigm, merely perpetuate an ostensibly benign *law of the jungle* in so far as nothing is shared equally. Such symbolic constructions as fairness, equality, and justice must manifestly *appear* as the banner of moral "Goodness" under which authority presides.

Although it *appears* impossible to share equally due to the complexities of subjectivity and subjective meaning, there's *nothing* prohibiting humans from a manifest will to equal Goodness and the pursuit thereof, other than our manifest will to Power *over* (Axiom 1).

Law

Rules are implicit within any symbolic system of meaning as there must be some middle ground (homeostasis, Axiom 28) of sense-making from which to act due to our subjectivity to other things and conditions.

Rules arise from discourses made possible because of symbolic language. Symbolic language itself relies upon rules of semantics and grammar in order to formulate meaning. The *political* and *supernatural paradigms of Power* represent innumerable symbolic discourses regulating who gets what under which conditions.

Although rules arise organically between agents pursuant to co-beneficial action, laws establish a *codified superstructure* of who gets what, when, how, and why. Both the political and supernatural paradigms represent purely *symbolic* "operating systems" lacking in substance (Axiom 13).

All symbolic systems are make-believe. The only paradigm of *substance* is the sexual paradigm (biological). Nothing objective occurs symbolically (although symbolic communication has very real consequences in *human-action*) as it is merely the realm of *form*.

The *sexual paradigm* represents our pre-symbolic evolution and our biological origin of Power (substance). From within this paradigm, we can imagine ourselves as existing in an objective world of substance, "logging onto" the "Internet" of symbolic meaning within the political and supernatural paradigms, and "downloading" the various "programs" which inform our daily *activities* within our substantive biological world.

However, *no* action in the (substantive) world of infrastructures, men, and machines has any *significance* outside of symbolic language. The political and supernatural paradigms (of meaning) *are* Power in the form of means (potentiality). As such, codified law is the highest (form) of Power in the political paradigm, while the master narratives of the supernatural paradigm, which *inform* codified law, are the *highest forms of Power* in our *Pyramid of Power*.

There are essentially five law forms regulating the Western hemisphere in addition to international maritime commercial law which are organized hierarchically from the bottom of our political paradigm as follows: *natural law, commercial* (contract) *law, common law, statutory law, political law,* and *admiralty/equity law.*

Natural law, originating at the base of the political paradigm, recognizes the agent as a product of nature (Axiom 23), and as such, having certain inalienable rights. Since the agent is ostensibly equipped by nature with sufficient mental and physical faculties to survive, he or she is endowed with the preponderance of being a responsible and sovereign being.

Commercial law (contract law), is based upon private self-determining, self-governing principles originating within natural law and is relevant to agent-to-agent contracts and agreements. *All* human interaction implicates *some* form of commercial (contract) law (explicit or implicit) which essentially takes the form of: *offer, acceptance, and ratification.* Since there is no longer any natural (meaningless) way of being in the world, everything we think, do, or say, is potentially an offer, e.g., the act of being born is an *offer* of new life to the symbol-using community. Since the right to life is symbolically codified and based in natural law, it is *accepted* that the individual should be allowed to live. *Permitting* the individual to live thus becomes *ratification* of the contract.

Stepping onto a public sidewalk is an offer to use the sidewalk according to common rules of etiquette, i.e., no cartwheeling, tumbling, littering, etc. Insofar as no one resists the act of using the public thoroughfare, it becomes tacit acceptance therein. Continued use of the sidewalk in accordance with the rules constitutes ratification of the *implied* contract.

Entering a public domain *implies* the right of an individual to solicit (contract with) others for any lawful purpose, whereupon a respondent may either accept or reject a given offer. In the event the offer were to "donate toward a worthy cause" and the respondent capitulates, it becomes tacit ratification of the contract.

Entering a restaurant is an offer to acknowledge the edifice as a public place of business. Waiting to be seated or seating oneself implies an offer to conduct business *and* to compensate the owner-proprietor fairly. Being served constitutes acceptance of the offer on behalf of the proprietor, and consuming the fare constitutes ratification on behalf of the patron, at which point the proprietor will create an *explicit* offer in the form of a bill. All law implicates some form of offer, acceptance, and ratification. In the event an offer is rejected, no contract is formed. Within public law where the "offer" is codified, acceptance is implied through the agreement of the people, therefore rejection of a public offer (statute) constitutes *dishonor* of a contract and therefore implies some form of penalty.

Common law is based upon the old English "law of the Commoners" (law of dispute and precedence) adopted around the signing of the Magna Carta which includes civil law and relates to matters arising between private agents but has been subsumed under the *color of* admiralty/equity/military law.

Statutory law is written law as a matter of public policy and is subordinate to common law. The sovereign individual is not compelled by statutory law, but rather contracts into it through various agreements usually in return for public benefits such that if the individual is seen as a receiver and/or acceptor of said benefits, the individual is liable and answerable to the demands of the laws (also subsumed under *color of law*).

Political law governs the intersection of law and politics, i.e., the law of the lawmakers, governing *who gets what* (subsumed under *color of law*, i.e., admiralty/equity law).

Maritime/admiralty/equity/military law is based upon ancient maritime laws governing commerce on the high seas and is comprised of *private international law*. Although it is superseded by contract and civil law (*law of the land*), it is a form of law which can be contracted into, thus overlaying contract law (as color of law) as a form of *trust law*. For example, a ship's captain traditionally assumed the role of trustee for passengers and property since the law of the land has no jurisdiction upon the high seas and since shipping is a risky proposition, thus (*formal*) contracts were created which entrusted passengers and cargo to the stewardship of the ship's captain (legal *agreements* as opposed to *lawful* contracts).

Passengers gave up certain lawful rights of the land in exchange for overseas transport and thus became the grantors to, and beneficiaries of, the ship's captain who represented ultimate authority according to the laws of the sea. Once passengers arrived safely on land, debts were settled *substantively*, jurisdiction of the sea was dissolved, and any lawful rights of the land restored to the passengers.

Traditionally, disclosure of a contract is not required within trust law as an individual is not compelled by trust law but rather contracts into it similar to hiring a babysitter wherein parents (grantors) contract with the sitter (trustee) to safeguard their children (beneficiaries) over a period of time. Herein, there is an agreement between the grantors and the trustee to watch over the best interests of the beneficiaries who then become subject to the authority of the trustee without full disclosure of any lawful relationship between them.

Since shipping was traditionally a risky proposition and commodities were often lost at sea due to piracy or a ship's sinking, *formal* (Axiom 13) agreements were exchanged in lieu of *substance* (it is more risky and costly to carry bulky substances, i.e., gold, silver, etc. aboard ship) such as bills of exchange, promissory notes, and other negotiable instruments.

Hence, law of the sea is a *formal* type of law as opposed to *substantive* law of the land. Substantive settlement occurs on land where commodities and infrastructures of exchange exist, while formal contracts are made at sea where it is neither safe nor practicable to settle substantively.

Law (as a major locus of the regulatory motive of *control*) warrants further elucidation since it is ostensibly the highest *form* of Power in the political paradigm. Therefore, although we have attempted to organize law forms hierarchically within our political paradigm from the more substantive near the bottom to the more formal near the top, there is an inverse relationship of Power (Axiom 5) in that in the absence of *living humans* on the land conducting commerce between themselves through the exchange of substantive commodities, formal contracts would be meaningless. Inversely, in the absence of formal spoken or written contracts, the law of the jungle would dominate as we revert to the sexual paradigm of Power since symbolic language must necessarily supersede human action within a *meaningful* world (Axiom 14).

Natural and commercial law, as delineated within the *Bill of Rights* and the *Constitution of the United States* supersedes common, statutory, political, and maritime law, in proportion to the people's ability to *know the law and be well-disposed to use it*, i.e., to be able to *respond* and *stand under*, their lawful rights of the land.

However, maritime or admiralty/equity law manifests itself as dominant in the world due to the Power of technology (Axiom 25) and a *common* incapacity of the people for standing under and responding to principles of *substance* due to ignorance and apathy, since those already in possession of Power (Axiom 9) control the levers of technology, i.e., meaning, i.e., belief, i.e., *reality*.

Since we are merely giving *critical voice* according to a particular standpoint (a *duty* to self and *obligation* to humanity) herein and *not* constructing a comprehensive historical affidavit of fact with respect to law *or any other loci of motives* and merely exploring "gravities" of "Truth" *as they are perceived*, it is necessary to condense a plethora of readily available knowledge into a more succinct chronology of events with respect to admiralty law since *color of law* has become the dominant form of law by default within our political paradigm (Axiom 1).

Therefore, with the rise of shipping (technology), previously organic and sacred connections between humans and the land became commodified and secular as the world became colonized under the banner of empire (Axiom 1). For example, the United States of America, formerly a sovereign jurisdiction of the private East India (Trading) Company formed for the purposes of *commercial* exploitation of the Americas, began as one such enterprise.

Although there were those who later emigrated in order to escape certain oppressions and to seek a better (Good) life, the origin of the United States was based on the will to Power *over* rather than moral "Goodness." The *private* commercial interests of the initial entrepreneurs predominated and arguably remain to this day.

We may, at this juncture, set aside whatever morass of private, corporate, legal, and lawful structures existed with respect to the United States before the time of the *revolution* and assume that if *enough* people (Axiom 18) contract according to *natural* and *commercial* laws of the land and *fight* to defend them, those individuals obtain lawful sovereignty upon the land.

However, even though sovereignty in America was obtained on behalf of the efforts of a *fraction* of the people, other interests were ostensibly at stake in the form of US Revolutionary War debt to France which was later subsumed by King George III and his financiers due to the debt of the French Revolutionary War.

Following Old Testament biblical canon concerning indebtedness, e.g., "Let your fields remain fallow in the seventh year," and penalties for disobedience therein, "Ten times seven," etc., the international financiers who now owned the American Revolutionary War debt began demanding payment.

First demand occurring in 1789—ostensibly seven years after it had been incurred—at which time, the relatively weak central government of America became bankrupt to the international bankers due to the refusal of the several states to pay (the debtor is slave to the lender). Upon the insistence of surety for the debt on behalf of the international financiers, the founding fathers created a contract *constituting* the debt of the now corporate US. Uncommon reading of this document according to *lawful* meaning of the day reveals the incorporation of the several sovereign United States of America into the U.S. corporation. A "constitutor" was one who constituted the debt of another as a lawful contract. Thus the Constitution of the "United States" constituted the debt of *the central government* to the international financiers. No *lawful* rights were given therein which didn't already exist according to natural and commercial law, therefore, the Constitution of the United States represents a corporate organizational charter which delineates *allowable* boundaries of action within the US corporation and a bond securing the debt of the central government to the international financiers.

Following Old Testament punitive canon of "ten times seven," the international financiers again demanded repayment of the Revolutionary War debt in 1859. This time, the Northern States approached the sovereign Southern States to underwrite the debt. The sovereign Southern States refused, and instead fought to preserve their sovereignty. (The civil war was fought over sovereignty, not slavery, which was already in decline. Lincoln was publicly unequivocal in his manifest objective to preserve the Union - not to end slavery.) The loss of the Civil War by the Southern States constituted the loss of the sovereignty (dishonor) of the several states and bankruptcy to the central government, a dishonor which has left John Q. Public in a perpetual "state of war" with the now federal government, as per the (still relevant) Lieber Code of 1863.

Seventy years hence, another call for liquidity in 1929 together with another dishonor precipitated the loss of the sovereignty of *the people* in addition to the loss of substance *in the public* (the loss of control of *substantive* wealth in 1933 as the gold standard was repealed in the *United States*, and the New Deal was implemented).

It was the loss of *substantive* wealth as the basis of *lawful* money which precipitated the Great Depression, *not* unregulated banking practices. An uncommon analysis reveals a veritable plethora of codified changes coinciding with the bankruptcy of 1929 with respect to the *lawful* individual, including creation of the dead corporate "PERSON" with whom the living *(substantive)* individual is held to be responsible in the public (democracy).

Although *the people* were bankrupted in 1929 and therefore lost substance in the public (democracy), they retain all lawful rights in the private (republic) since lawful rights, by nature, cannot be taken away.

The New Deal introduced an extraordinary aggregate of *formal* policies in the public (democracy) designed to enslave the living individual to the debt of the international financiers while obfuscating the lawful private rights of the individual (in the republic) via a two-trust system, i.e., one which allows private lawful individuals to *voluntarily* contract into becoming corporate receivers of public benefits (citizen-slaves within the jurisdiction of the democracy).

Many *formal* artifices were created such as those which delineated the agreements which provided for such creations, i.e., *House Joint Resolution 192, Publication 1212, Modern Money Mechanics,* and *generally accepted accounting practices (GAAP),* etc., and those which created the formal contracts, i.e., birth certificates, Social Security cards, driver's licenses, etc.

The most recent bankruptcy of 1999 precipitated the loss of all *lawful* rights (i.e., *substantive* wealth) of *the people* in the public (democracy) equating to the biblical transfer from the *wooden,* to the *iron* yoke of slavery, precipitating the Great Recession of 2008 (Axiom 28).

From an uncommon-sense perspective, the movie *The Matrix* (Wachowski, Andy and Larry), released in 1999, is a thinly disguised analog to the contemporary social implications of this most recent bankruptcy, containing therein a veritable plethora of explicit metaphors relating to the theme of slave versus master and digits becoming SS numbers on the program's homepage.

Indeed, a veritable plethora of excerpts, books, movies, and media attesting to a continual subsummation of natural and commercial law by trust law, i.e., admiralty/equity law (as color of law/money) is readily available to the uncommon-sense maker, e.g., *The Creature from Jekyll Island* (G. Edward Griffin), Publication 1212, *Modern Money Mechanics* (Federal Reserve Bank of Chicago), *Debt Virus* (Jacques S. Jaikaran), UCC, *The Wonderful Wizard of Oz* (L. Frank Baum), CFR Section V, *Black's Law Dictionary (lawful* definitions pre- and post-bankruptcies), *The Federalist Papers,* etc.

At the close of the US Constitutional Convention on September 17, 1787, as Benjamin Franklin left Constitution Hall in Philadelphia, he was asked, "What kind of government have you given us, Dr. Franklin?" To which he replied, "A republic - *if you can keep it.*"

The history of admiralty/equity law is a history of knowledge (of technique) of commerce, banking, and legal structure which is a knowledge of *form* over *substance*. When substance is *abandoned,* it is subsumed formally. This process began with the invention of the symbol wherein he who controls the symbols controls meaning, he who controls meaning controls belief, and he who controls belief controls (constructs) reality (Axiom 11), e.g., within the ancient Mayan cultures of Central America, only the elite could understand the sacred symbols which preserved their hegemony.

A *commonsense* approach to law reveals a naturalized, inevitable, and necessary substructure created *by* the Good of society *for* the Good of society. However, in Western society, law (the most fundamental and significant field of study after communication) is magnificently missing from the *public* curriculum as an essential course of study in primary education and remains obscure throughout secondary education *unless* it is specifically chosen as a course of study. The obscurity of law, as the highest expression of symbolic meaning, is preserved through its arcane and esoteric practices and symbols apart from commonsense knowledge (Axiom 9).

An uncommon-sense approach towards sense-making reveals law as an ancient practice steeped in occultic traditions spanning thousands of years of history and dominion. For example, the ceremonial "robe of Saturn" worn by judges as members of the BAR (British Attorney Registry); the use of archaic Latin (legalese) as the official language of law and the symbolic structure of a courtroom as a ship upon which litigants ceremoniously enter as if upon the bridge thereof, thereby abandoning any *lawful* rights of the land and giving the judge jurisdiction over their *private lawful rights* as the ship's captain with his or her gold-fringed flag of admiralty displayed in the background.

Additionally, for the majority of those entering the practice of law (ostensibly through traditions of nepotism and class [Axioms 4 and 9] as in other highly *public* occupations) in the bankrupt state-owned institutions of higher education, future practitioners acquire only a *formal* introduction to natural and commercial law with emphasis centered in corporate, statutory, and trust law, i.e., *color of law* under admiralty/equity.

There is less compensatory reward in defending an individual's lawful (as opposed to "legal") rights, which for the most part have been abandoned by default, and much greater opportunity servicing the ever expanding world of corporate and statutory law. The majority of *persons* in the Western hemisphere are born utterly ignorant and irresponsible (Axiom 10) in terms of their *lawful* rights and ostensibly prefer to clamor in huddled masses in order to become citizen-slave, receivers of meager benefits in the public (democracy).

In sum, laws are the ultimate codified rules of engagement within symbolic language. No *meaningful* action is possible outside of symbolic language and no organizational structure exists without some form of law. As such, law is the arbiter of *Power,* and the most dominant form is the most *Powerful.*

The concept of law as a mechanism of justice ("Good") rather than operating system for Power is counterintuitive, e.g., equality is construed to be "Good," yet humans do not practice equality independent of the law, and law is created *by* humans, so there must be an ulterior motive other than "Good" which prevails since humans do not practice equality "naturally" without ulterior reward. And there *cannot be* equality if some humans are *necessarily* empowered over others so as to ensure equality.

The same applies to any form of "justice," i.e., the "Good" which is being sought is sought because it was lacking *initially*. It is *from* this overall *pool of lack* (deficit) which we somehow formulate higher Goods (credits) which then can be used to ensure fairness. However, the initial state *was* a state of lack, therefore the manufacturing of additional "Goodness" creates an even greater deficit, and therefore *voluntary servitude* and increased dependency upon "superior" sources of "justice."

The energy required to satiate said lack of Goodness is extracted from the common-sense-making "goyim" and consolidated at a higher level (as Power over), thus the Pyramid of Power grows upward and evermore concentrated near the top (Axioms 1, 8, and 9). What was missing initially was *fair and equal* empowerment practiced purely in the name of *Goodness*. Thus the cycle continues.

If the *manifest* motive of all humans was *equally shared* Goodness, there would be no need for law. Therefore, law preserves a (politically correct and codified) manifest will to Power *over* (Axiom 1) concealed behind curtains of ambiguity and "Goodness," i.e., as per *The Wonderful Wizard of Oz*.

Government

If all men *were* equal, then government would be meaningless as all would be equally maintained pursuant to the Good. It is due to the fact that men are *not* equal that governments exist. It is a human embarrassment that governments promote "equality" through public policy. Ensuring equality through mandatory hiring practices in the public is analogous to saying that, these, our employees, are amongst those whom we officially consider less "equal," but now *are* equal *because* we hired them. Such practices seem rather to institutionalize social inequality.

If men are neither "created" nor equal in nature, dominance arises due to: biological advantage, differential circumstances of birth, and symbolic hierarchy. Evolution *is* a paradigm of hierarchy between and within species and between the dominant and submissive, as in human social hierarchy.

To govern is to *control*, i.e., to regulate, to *dominate*, regardless of type of social structure, e.g., clan, tribe, republic, democracy, etc. However, there must necessarily exist *some* hierarchical benefit within the political and supernatural paradigms, therefore the political paradigm is the paradigm of *who gets what*, and consecrated as authoritative and therefore "Good" within the supernatural paradigm. Therefore, all men must necessarily be re-*created* as equal through *supernatural* authority since we are not equal by human-evolutionary standards.

There are essentially two models for the origin of government: one arises organically as humans interact under a common purpose, and one arises as a result of Powerful interests. Whether organic or

a result of Powerful interests, governments necessarily exist to preserve and protect rights which are necessarily implicated in Power
relationships.

In the Powerful interests model, the very concept of inequality
is the core structure of government, e.g., a wealthy landowner or dic-
tator structures his or her administration so as to preserve the status
quo of his or her position of dominance.

Within collectivist cultures more egalitarian forms of government are possible, yet due to multiple subjectivities (Axioms 21 and
5) it is impossible to share *all* resources equally even in the absence of
an inclination toward dominance (Axioms 3 and 5).

The evolution of political Power ostensibly began within more
or less egalitarian tribal societies, e.g., an evolutionary cross section
of our Pyramid of Power just above the sexual paradigm would most
likely reveal a more egalitarian and less hierarchical sampling of the
distribution of Power amongst the masses than today.

Governments form since it is not our natural inclination to share
equally, and it is ostensibly impossible to share equally *in time* due
to subjectivity. Knowledge tends to be retained and shared predominantly within special interest groups, i.e., families, corporations, and
governments, etc. Knowledge of technique *is* Power, and unequal
knowledge *assures* unequal Power (Axioms 8 and 9).

Technology and Power go hand in hand and are hierarchical-
the more knowledge one wields, the less subject one is to resistance
in pursuit of her or his Good and thus rises within the Pyramid of
Power (Appendix III). Since Power begets power (Axiom 9), more
empowered individuals become increasingly capable of rising still
further in pursuit of their own Good.

Thus, it is human nature to ascend hierarchically due to the
pollution and *purification* of symbolic meaning (see Burke's pollu-
tion/purification). Governments are composed of humans and thus
are equally predisposed toward *purification*, i.e., empowerment.
Governments not only compete with their citizenry for Power and
control, but with other governments and political adversaries.

Post-symbolic human evolution represents a hierarchical evolution of technical knowledge, the peak thereof representing the pinna-

cle of technical knowledge which increases exponentially in relation to the empowering factors of technology. Within such a model, we should expect to observe an ever increasing disparity of knowledge (Power) between ruling classes and their subjects, which ostensibly appears to be the case as evidenced by innumerable public and private sources.

In the United States, the period of time when the law (of the land) was passed from father to son *privately*, and the people more or less knew the law *and were well-disposed to use it*, has become a time in which government and law are simply too complex and nebulous for common-sense reasoning.

Whereas a typical, responsible landowner *might* have filled the shoes of a president in a more *lawful* time, there are very few lawful landowners and a majority of "legal" paper owners who are but mere "tenants upon the land" - which is "under water." Due to voluntary indebtedness, the US citizen-slave has become subsumed within a matrix of formal "legal" obligations under de facto law of the sea and a de facto government.

Law (of the land), which was once unambiguous and comprehensible, has been subsumed under *color of law* as admiralty/equity law and become so technical and complex that even experienced practitioners must specialize in particular species and subspecies of law (Axiom 25). Even *if* the average citizen had the time *and* resources to study and become a guru of all law forms, in the United States, she/he would merely rediscover herself/himself as a *dead corporate entity devoid of any lawful rights in the public* and owning more debt than she/he or her/his fellow citizens, or generations thereof, could ever repay.

Law form dictates policy and political action, and whatever actions are occurring publicly, implicates which forms of law are being adhered to. A republican form of law preserves the *individual* as a more or less autonomous and responsible sovereign entity of lawful rights.

In relation to more or less responsible and sovereign citizens, governments assume a less active role as an agency regulating human interaction and commerce and therefore are not as often invoked, thus fewer laws and offices of governance are required and fewer regulatory devices, e.g., licenses, registrations (regis = king, terre = territory, i.e., jurisdiction of a king), certifications, *formal* documents, etc.

As long as an individual causes no harm nor interferes with the rights of another, or in such cases where individuals exercise their *capacity* to settle matters quickly between them, there is no *lawful* cause for governmental intervention. Under such a form, one would expect to witness a relatively small and laissez-faire government with relatively few restrictions or requirements.

A democratic form of government places less emphasis on individual rights than on public rights and assumes that what is "Good" for the public must be in the best interests of the individual. Since the individual cannot be entrusted to be his "brother's keeper," it is necessary that a strong government exists to ensure equality for everyone. Under this form of law, a government is invoked as a *necessary* intermediary between the Powerful and less Powerful, thus many assurances must be put in place in order to control and regulate human interaction and commerce.

Since individuals are not viewed as responsible for their own actions and behaviors, common and trust laws are evoked as dominant over natural and commercial law. Thus citizens become a commodity or property for which the government becomes responsible as the *trustee*, and thus many regulatory assurances and safety precautions must be enacted, e.g., licenses, registrations, certifications, *formal* (corporate) agreements, etc.

Under this form of law, governments and bureaucracies *must* mediate between persons who abandon responsibility by default. Here one would expect to witness a ubiquitous government at every level of human interaction, including all manner of mandatory licenses and permits, many restrictions and statutes governing nearly all human interactions, a great degree of surveillance and monitoring, and many fees and taxes in order to support a Leviathan of bureaucracy.

One might also expect such a form of government to flourish as private interests atrophy and fees and regulations increase in response to bureaucratic complexity. And since humans by nature are not fair and equitable, one would expect to witness a spiral of taxing and spending as hierarchical governmental interests transformed the private *substantial* interests of the people into the *formal* public political interests of the government.

Governments necessarily restrict liberties under the guise of maintaining equality and preserving *security*, however, many such "threats" which evoke changes in policy or restrict civil liberties remain as nebulous in their origins and causes as the morass of *statutes* which are ostensibly created on their behalf.

Due to the subjectivity of language and meaning and the contradictions which arise therein (Axioms 3, 14, and 15), governments seek to establish authority through *divine* association, e.g., *the divine right of kings*, and through such concepts as men being *endowed* with certain inalienable rights by virtue of a *creator* (an alignment copacetic to a commonsense orientation steeped in tradition and superstition).

In sum, one could spend several lifetimes analyzing, writing, and expounding upon the histories, philosophies, and complexities of government since *control*, in the guise of regulation (safety, security, predictability, efficacy, etc.), is a most basic motive in evolution (Appendix IV) as well as the political and the supernatural paradigms, where authorities exercise ultimate control over human destiny within the political paradigm of who gets what.

Control is diametrically opposed to *subjectivity*, the condition which is the basis of all motives. Any subsequent topic of analysis is merely a subspecies of control, e.g., control of assets, control of social status, control of self, control over self-empowerment, etc. Control provides the foundation for *synthesis* and thus higher potential Power *over* subjectivity (Appendices I and II).

Governments exist since humans (Axioms 23 and 26) are naturally predisposed to self-preservation over species preservation—yet are symbolically interdependent (Axioms 4 and 17) due to the organizational technology of language. Society as we know it could not exist for symbol-using animals without some framework of organization and individuals appointed to regulate it. There is indeed much Good within a regulated society as opposed to the law of the jungle, and most, if not all law is created under *some* auspice of manifest "Good." However, the concept of government would be irrelevant if equal Goodness was our dominant motive. The motive of control is manifestly about our *will to Power over* (Appendix I).

Policy Enforcement

Depending on the nature of law and government, what constitutes the status of a citizen in relation to its government, and therefore it's lawful status, could be graphed dialectically between the extremities of slave/despotism on one side, and sovereign/self-governing at the other.

On a political continuum a democracy would be composed more of citizen-slaves and a despotic government and appear as a polar opposite to a republic composed of sovereign self-governing individuals. If the basic assumption of a democratic form of government is that everyone should have *equal* voice but do not due to Powerful interests and therefore a formidable third-party *must be invoked* as an arbiter (trustee) of equality, then the nature of this structure is not dissimilar to that of a day care school for children insofar as said children are viewed as irresponsible in looking after their own best interests—in the absence of a parent or legal guardian—*and* require indoctrination *as* beneficiaries of the trustee as how to best interact according to principles of equality and civic duty.

If the basic assumption of a republican form of government is that everyone is free to become and do whatever they wish according to their inalienable rights *as long as they do not injure another nor another's property,* and in the event of controversy, have the capacity to respond quickly (be response-able) and provide a remedy, then the nature of this structure must be one which *assumes* individuals to be responsible and willing to accept *responsibility.*

In the latter case, the role of the government is more laissez-faire with respect to individual liberties and commerce and invoked only in the most exigent of cases. The individual would remain sovereign and free as long as she/he controlled her/his assets and "avoided incurring liabilities in the form of damages to others.

Although even a cursory overview of law was majestically absent from the *public* curriculum of *this* writer during his indoctrination as a citizen, his perceived *historical* perspective of US history was ostensibly more reflective of the qualities of a *republican* form of governance, e.g., *life, freedom, liberty, independence, responsibility, strength, equality, justice, natural rights,* etc.

Every perceivable indication is that the founders of the United States *of America* conformed *more* to a profile of self-governing sovereigns than that of codependent corporate slaves. From the *standpoint* of this writer, the ideals represented by those founding fathers and implicated in the American Revolution have been utterly inverted insofar as *living* individuals are not publicly recognized as such by their government and "freedom" has become a *hollow signifier* as opposed to a human right, and, insofar as poverty is equal to Liberty as the only *legal* alternative to voluntary servitude, and independence is equal to homelessness and banishment from public commerce.

Independence of mind is perhaps most contrary to a democratic structure since independent thinking may lead to *uncommon* ideas such as: "How might the founding fathers of the United States *of America*, if alive today, respond to the current state of personal liberty and independence?"

If, as it *appears* from within the social orientation of this writer that the United States and other contemporary (de facto) governments are decidedly more on the side of the despotism/slave dialectic, then the US founding fathers, if alive today, *might* discover they have no *lawful* rights in the public (democracy), and that the airing of grievances and pursuit of redress may constitute "terrorism" and or treason under such statutes as the "Patriot" Act where the *wooden* yoke of slavery under the despotism of King George III has become the *iron* yoke (post-1999).

The form of government under which an individual acts is usually evident in the presence (or lack thereof) of its constabulary. Although it might be difficult to imagine a contemporary society lacking in the presence of policy enforcers (police), there exist examples within living memory of smaller communities which neither had need of a constabulary nor need of invoking neighboring constabularies.

The lack of constabulary presence in the above example is not indicative of a lack of multiple layers of government, but of what may and may not invoke their presence, e.g., people generally getting along and acting responsibly and a lack of significant commercial activity.

It is possible to imagine a sizable town or even city with minimal to no presence of a constabulary wherein all citizens act responsibly (Axiom 4). However, in relation to increasing size and complexity, it is easy to imagine many conflicts of interest arising, and therefore a necessity for additional agreements (rules) with a corresponding increase in policy enforcers.

Even with additional rules (policies, laws), it seems *possible* for individuals to act responsibly and avoid and mediate conflict themselves to a significant degree (Axiom 27), and that under such a system, there would be no need for imposing penalties except in cases where *damages* were sustained or some form of *harm* was inflicted due to negligence.

Under the form of policy enforcement above, one would not perceive a *manifest* police presence the constabulary would only respond within a prescribed jurisdiction and only when invoked due to an instance of *property damage* or *personal harm*.

Working from the assumption that a democratic form of government is *more* proactive in regulating the affairs of its citizenry and that its citizenry is assumed to be, to some degree, irresponsible in its affairs, one might expect to witness an omni-presence of policy enforcers and perhaps even a sense reverence for such an "ant upon aphid" relationship.

Such a proactive and ubiquitous constabulary is in fact what appears to be the case at least in western societies indicating a very "blue-shifted" democratic form of government, e.g., a ubiquitous police presence on public thoroughfares, ubiquitous monitoring of public and private activities, and warrantless access to public and *private* commercial transactions and records.

If we were to locate the early form of government propounded by the founding fathers of the United States *of America*, upon our imaginary government/citizen dialectical scale, it would ostensibly be located very near the extremity of the self-governing/sovereign (republican) form of governance, while contemporary forms would be equally shifted toward the despot/slave (democratic) form of governance.

However, all words and symbols are *hollow signifiers,* which, over time, become imbued with new meanings as a method of altering perception and therefore, belief (Axioms 11 and 16). Someone who was once revered and honored as a "patriot" thereby becomes a "terrorist." The ambiguity of symbols enables broad, sweeping categorizations of meaning—a favorable condition for the consolidation of Power. However, the less *authoritatively* defined a word or symbol, the less *lawful* it is.

Most assuredly, the words *democracy* and *republic* have been imbued with a veritable plethora of meanings throughout history, however, even though they remain authoritatively defined today, they have ostensibly digressed, due to a common-sense orientation to sense-making (Axiom 12), into parochial catchphrases of "representing the working class" or "big business," respectively.

However, no matter which party is more empowered, there is ostensibly *no* change in the presence of the constabulary nor in its surveillance practices. In fact, not much appears to change in the public at all other than a continuous (non-partisan) increase in policies and restrictions.

In relation to the omnipresence of surveillance and the constabulary, one might, from an *uncommon-sense* point of view wonder: Whose policies are being enforced? Particularly, when one doesn't recall agreeing to or voting on a plethora of fees, taxes, and statutes which by all appearances *shouldn't* be necessary and ostensibly erode away at life, liberty, and the pursuit of happiness (King George III only extracted about 5 percent of the colonies' wealth, whereas today it is closer to 65 percent).

If we are correct in our assessments regarding international debts and obligations, it becomes evident (as proposed above) that whatever policies are enforced publicly must necessarily represent the best *interest* of international financiers to whom debts are owed, both public and private, within a bankrupt society.

Thus, it would appear to make little difference which political party is empowered as long as the *interests* of the creditors are met. *If* this were true, a socialist type of government makes sense—in which the governments assume control over their bankrupt and irresponsible citizens through the creation of "dead" corporate entities through which they can extract energy from the *living individual* through mandated licenses, registrations, taxes, permits, and fees in exchange for meager public benefits.

Likewise, from an uncommon-sense perspective, one might puzzle over massive military-industrial complexes and their specific purposes. A common-sense purpose would seem to be to protect and defend the rights of their *citizenry*. However, what are their legal and *lawful* functions and duties, and what right, if any, does the citizen have of disclosure thereof?"

If there are specific and basic policies which invoke military action, it would be elucidating to learn of them so as to better understand (stand under) and appreciate what measure of security one is actually acquiring *and* entitled to from their armed forces in relation to the costs thereof. If the people and their children's children must bear the perpetual cost of a standing army, one might suppose that the people would be sufficiently vested as to acquire an uncommon-sense perspective in relation to just how massive of a standing army is required as well as the specific nature of any perceived threats to their nation's security.

It seems reasonable that if a country is sufficiently large and in possession of vast resources, a large military establishment is necessary in order to protect its borders, civilians, and resources. Moreover, it is understandable that a military must exercise some degree of opaqueness (from the civilian population) as a matter of national security.

However, in relation to an ostensible ambiguity associated with military *purpose*, an uncommon-sense orientation reveals a ubiquitous public *reverence* and *homage* thereto through innumerable public and media rhetoric. Extraordinary pomp, circumstance, and recognition is attributable to all things military or constabulary as though policy enforcers and their respective agencies represent all that is Good and righteous.

From an uncommon-sense perspective, a necessity for policy enforcers is a *sign* (Axiom 16) of manifest human *unwillingness* to share equally (otherwise we wouldn't *require* policies), as such, the role (job, occupation) of policy enforcers is a necessary "evil," since such jobs must necessarily be created to enforce the "Good."

Additionally, policymakers and enforcers do not produce *substantive* value for society, and therefore ultimately create additional burden upon the people. However, in a slave (democracy) society, such policy-oriented occupations and organizations instead represent a surrogate source of *pride* to the people rather than a necessary "evil" (for the *utilitarian* purpose of defense and security) from which one might *otherwise* turn one's gaze (as per the eagle on the great seal of the United States which faces *away* from the *utilitarian* implements of war clutched in its *left* talons and *toward* the olive branch of *peace*).

Indeed, *once* respectable men had the following to say—

James Madison:
The means of defense against foreign danger, have always been the instruments of tyrannies at home. Among the Romans it was a standing maxim to incite a war, whenever a revolt was apprehended. Throughout all Europe, the armies kept up under pretext of defending, have enslaved the People.

Samuel Adams:
Such a professional army was always dangerous to the liberties of the people.

Similar pomp, circumstance, and reverence ostensibly surrounded the colonial British military (whose allegiance was *to the king*) amongst loyalists right up until the time of the Boston Massacre (and presumably thereafter), which was instrumental in fomenting the American Revolution. Two hundred years later, students at a US university were gunned down in similar fashion culminating in one less death and three more injuries at the hands of policy enforcers *whose job was ostensibly to protect them and their rights* (including freedom of speech). That incident now seems only a blip in the continuum of history by comparison, as do the many who fought for and defended such obsolete ideals as liberty, justice, freedom, independence, etc.

A paradox of governments and law (as institutions of *protection,* i.e., "Good") is that their ultimate Power resides in *violence.* Whether a given policy is just, or even *lawful,* is less a matter of fact than the penal machinations (Power) from which it was constructed (Axioms 1, 3, 4, and 5).

In sum, since humans are not moral (Good) by nature and seek "Goodness" *through* empowerment (Axioms 1, 21, 23, and 26), rules and laws arise as organized methods of determining who gets what. Since laws (policies) are enacted by humans whose *manifest* motive is self-interest, they are both manifestly and latently all about Power *over.*

Just as laws (policies) are necessary to an ordered and structured society, so too are those required to enforce them who are likewise manifestly motivated by Power *over—unless* there are those unbeknownst to this writer who volunteer their services without remuneration according to a manifest motive of Good, i.e., protecting and defending human rights to life, liberty, and the pursuit of property and happiness *and* sharing in them *equally.*

All who work and participate in the organization, production, and administration of a *great society* ought to be revered and commended as *equal* under the maxim, "All men are equal," *unless* some (men) are going above and beyond their job description and *volunteering* their services and putting their lives in peril. *These should be revered above all,* but only *if* the people they are serving are presumed to have the *right to know* what *in fact* said volunteers are presumed to be protecting and defending *in their names* and upon what grounds, and *in fact* are given such explicit knowledge.

From an uncommon-sense point of view, it *seems* inequitable and nonsensical to honor and revere *any* individual or organization above others solely based upon its title or *perceived* nobility. *Unless* the motive for such tribute-giving to such species of the "emperor's new clothes" is to align oneself with the emperor's Power *over*, in which case it seems merely inequitable.

However, for those individuals who *have* volunteered, *or* been conscripted, paid or not, with a manifest *motive* of Good, i.e., *protecting and serving* life, liberty, equality, and the pursuit of property and happiness for living individuals and have sacrificed life and limb *believing* as much—*these ought to be honored above all!*

The original Thirteenth Amendment to the US Constitution provided for the abolishment of titles of nobility in the republic, however, following the bankruptcy of 1859 and the war over *sovereignty*, i.e., the Civil War, which was lost, thus invoking yet another level of US bankruptcy, the Thirteenth Amendment was changed to read "no *involuntary* servitude" in the *democracy*. Thus re-establishing British legal authority and nobility in the US democracy and the presence of imperial titles of nobility *under color of law* e.g., admiral, ensign, etc.(military), and esquire (as a member of the British attorney registry).

If there were any indication of what *form* of government an individual is subject to, it should become evident in the rituals and practices (Axiom 16) of the policy enforcers, public officials, and in the revery held for such positions in the public. Policy is determined by those in Power (Axiom 9), and policy enforcement protects both the *manifest* and *latent* interests of those in *Power*.

Citizenship

The individual has both a historical and a structural orientation to his or her location within the political paradigm. As a historical figure, everything the political paradigm represents is the net result of an extensive evolution of symbolic interactions between individuals. In contemporary terms, the individual is suspended and therefore subsumed (Axiom 25) within the symbolic matrix according to location within the paradigm.

The contemporary *role* of the individual is significant to the motive of control since it is only through roles that we are enabled to interact meaningfully as socially-symbolic beings. The fundamental role of most contemporary individuals is that of citizen of a nation, state, or commonwealth.

A citizen is a legally or lawfully recognized subject or national of a particular political order. Whatever a citizen is capable of doing or becoming lawfully or legally, is dependent upon its form of government and laws.

On a global scale, governments around the world appear to be evolving toward democratic or socialistic forms of governance, i.e., a *"New World Order,"* as opposed to sovereign orthodox republics. If so, global citizens are evolving away from a *substantive* existence (particularly post-Industrial Revolution), toward a *formal* one (Axiom 13).

Less than two hundred years ago in the United States, Native Americans predominantly lived off the land and traded in commodities which had intrinsic value. Today, those which remain are subsumed within *form*al treaties restricting access to traditional lands (*substance*) and are constrained to the use of fiat monies and other purely *symbolic* forms of exchange.

European inhabitants do not provide as stark of an example of a shift from *substance* to *form* since those cultures have long since been creating *formal* contracts involving property and money, however, most of the early European settlers in the United States lived predominately off the land producing much of what they needed to survive themselves from the land.

The Industrial Revolution brought about significant changes throughout the Western world as people began exchanging more liquid forms of money and credit in return for modern conveniences which they couldn't produce themselves, however, credit was secured by commodities and money backed by *substance* such as gold and silver.

In the United States, the bankruptcy of 1929 effectively brought about the demise of *substantive* money and the people's loss of substance in the *public* on March 9, 1933. The corporate PERSON (citizen) was created as a means for the default government to lawfully contract with lawful living individuals upon the land as *legal* entities under GAAP, the UCC and *Modern Money Mechanics*.

Through the international financiers' impoundment of substantive wealth in the public and creation of a legal (private) fiat money system (see *The Creature from Jekyll Island*), they have been empowered to control the value of money by a process of—first inflation, then deflation, thereby "embezzling" value from fiat dollars at a current inflation rate of 2,270.9 percent. In this manner, energy is extracted from the lives of *living individuals* through a slow and steady symbolic devaluation (this *before* fees in the form of taxes, licenses, registrations, permits, etc.).

In sum, the living individual, who in cooperation with other living individuals constructed the *formal* system of *symbolic language*, has abandoned his/her *substance* (responsibility) and become subsumed (through a continuum of *formal* agreements) within a matrix of complexity as a *nonliving* entity with no *lawful* rights in the public (and ever fewer in the private) and is held as a bond for international indebtedness by the creation of the *birth certificate* thereby becoming a *"legalized" citizen-slave* (*voluntary* servitude) to the state in return for Social Security, and other public benefits.

Such a transfer of energy from the bottom of the PoP toward the top may be construed as "Good" if equal or greater value were being returned to the citizens. However, all *appearances* indicate that energy is being extracted wholesale and that said extraction increases over time, and that said energies *are not* returned for the benefit of the "great society," but instead constitute tribute paid according to the *interests* of the top of the pyramid.

Thus the "citizen" is a construct of the motive of *control*, and therefore a commodity in the *manifest will to Power over* (Axiom 1).

Public Education

In the United States, since all states are bankrupt to the federal government, which in turn is bankrupt to the international financiers, all public institutions operate according to the "legal" structure of the states as per the guidelines of the default federal government.

We say *"legal"* structure since *lawful* structure has been abandoned due to the various levels of bankruptcy and the un-response-ability of the people, therefore public institutions operate under *color of law article I, admiralty law* as a component of *private international maritime law* at the behest of private interests.

All public institutions of education naturally conform to the *interests* of the international creditors, i.e., commercial, legal, political, and allegiant. Therefore, a liberal, lawful, and critical education is replaced with a "politically correct" conservative and *form*-al "education" designed to produce a docile and compliant *common-sense* workforce.

Everything necessary to inculcate the role of a commercial *voluntary* citizen-servant is taught publicly beginning with primary education, i.e., reading, writing, arithmetic, allegiance, conformity, cooperation, identity, ritual, and *citizenship*, as opposed to a liberal education, i.e., philosophy, law, liberal history, theory, critical thinking, the arts, intuitivity, and *self-reliance*.

The rituals and symbols of the dominant (liberally educated) interests are proudly and ignorantly embraced by the common-sense initiate as recognition and reward for "achievement," i.e., placing of a *star* upon the forehead for learning or donning of the robe of Saffron (Saturn) and the Masonic mortarboard cap upon g-r-a-d-u-a-t-i-o-n, i.e., gradual induction into voluntary servitude.

Medical-Industrial Complex

As opposed to times and places in the world where a physician was paid only when the patient was made well, Western contemporary medicine is designed to keep individuals dependent upon its services and remedies. Doctors acquire indoctrination (*legal* right to practice) only through the public education system, where values and motives are inculcated, i.e., commercial and hierarchical.

The individual's indoctrination as a compliant citizen-slave and subsequent fallacious perception of the medical-industrial complex is that of a benevolent institution which exists for the best interests (Good) of the individual (although there are undoubtedly benevolent minded individuals within such institutions who have likewise been indoctrinated), however medical-industrial superstructure, as with public education, conforms to the motives of the dominant interests, i.e., commercial dominance under *color of law*.

The individual, indoctrinated as a dependent and un-re-sponse-able citizen, forgets that a state of health begins with the individual whose life choices ought to be as if there were no doctors and whose diagnosis' are initially incumbent upon the individual. This is not to suggest that individuals are solely responsible for any given condition which may arise (Axiom 17), nor that individuals always have the capability of self-treatment, but rather that a state of health (homeostasis) is very much a factor of the response-able individual.

Responsibility applies equally to "accidents." There are "acts of God," such as earthquakes or meteor showers, which individuals can do little to avoid or avert, and there are *irresponsibilities* which cul-minate in some form of damage. Most "accidents'"can be shown to be incidents of negligence, i.e., crossing a street without checking for traffic, failing to inspect a tool or device for defects, or *failure to reasonably analyze any proposed action in the first part*.

Rather than focusing on health and prevention, state-sanctioned medical-industrial complexes focus upon malady and treatment. It would be counterintuitive for such an enormous medical-industrial complex to promote a healthy lifestyle and prevent illness so as to undermine the revenue-generating machinery of such a multibil-lion-dollar industry. Profit margins of pharmaceutical corporations alone rival those of banks, whose only overhead is the theatrical pro-duction and props necessary to support the illusion of "money."

As per the common (Nietzscheian) "heard instinct," we flock to quasi-public institutions not because we understand their manifest purpose, motive, structure, or even chain of authenticity (Axioms 12 and 14), but because we are *indoctrinated* to do so (Axiom 12). Today, few individuals are even *born* without the aid, blessing, and commercial liability of a quasi-public institution.

The individual becomes confused (subsumed) between knowl-edge, technological achievement, "progress," authority, duty, and lawful right. Since we are indoctrinated from *birth* (as in the birthing of a new ship) that the state is *as it appears to be* and has ultimate authority and jurisdiction according to the law, it not only seems *nat-*

ural to indenture oneself to quasi-public institutions, but it also feels *Good* believing that such ostensibly well-ordered, clean, modern, and efficient, institutions exist *for the Good* of the individual.

What the individual is presented with within the medical-industrial complex is the Good side of the "sword of technology"—that which giveth, also taketh away. Technology may indeed be "Good" and represent "progress" in many respects, yet many *structural causes* of illness are ignored or downplayed, such as a poor diet and improper exercise due to irresponsibility and a preference for convenience.

As corporatized, nonliving, bankrupt citizen-slaves (roles which we ostensibly clamor for in huddled masses), it matters not how we chose to destroy ourselves (as long as it is politically correct) due to poor diet, stress, lack of exercise, substance abuse, lack of will, lack of esteem, lack of self-respect, lack of spirit, etc. All of these a manifestation of a mass exodus from *substance* to *form,* i.e., *responsibility* to *convenience.*

Throughout history, humans lived upon and worked the land. Foods were neither convenient nor processed, and people achieved adequate physical exercise by producing things for themselves (physical exercise naturally combats the negative effects of stress, and substances from the land are natural and devoid of synthetic chemicals, preservatives, or additives). Self-sufficiency and self-reliance are antonyms for lack of self-esteem and self-respect (persistent states of mind which are fertile ground for all manner of mental illness and substance abuse).

Alternatively, corporations exist solely for profit and present all manner of malady to the individual in exchange for convenience and irresponsibility. Individuals are enticed into becoming *consumers* of convenience and commercial entertainment. In exchange, we become economic instruments of *voluntary servitude* and are constrained to specialized jobs and tasks which become contradictory to a healthy lifestyle, therefore, due to having traded away our time (Axiom 29), we seek convenience in obtaining other things which we can no longer produce for ourselves, i.e., processed foods packaged and marketed for profit as opposed to nutrition and thrift.

Large corporations acquire large benefits within a bankrupt system devoid of substance (law). It is in the best interests of corporations to exploit the masses as consumers and laborers in the interest of profit. It is the interest of governments to acquire tribute from large corporations in exchange for the benefits and a "legal" right to do commerce within their jurisdictions.

If the medical-industrial complex's manifest goal was *health and prevention,* it would speak in opposition to corporate voluntary servitude, convenience, and all manner of known and discoverable structural causes of malady, (such as cancer with its multifarious connections with processed foods, chemicals, pollution, radiation, vaccines, etc.), i.e., structural corporate consumerism and convenience.

It is the irresponsible masses which clamor for convenience (*form* over *substance*) and nonresponsibility that enables default governments, kings, and voluntary servitude to arise. The institutions which arise in response manifestly and latently cater to the corporate and fiduciary interests of the dominant over those of the individual. The medical-industrial complex exists pursuant to the interests of the political paradigm in its manifest will to power *over.*

Quasi-Public Corporations

Contemporary corporations are legally "dead" entities which must conform to a plethora of regulations in order to acquire benefits as corporations within a bankrupt and fiat society. Shareholders' are shielded from various liabilities in the public while benefitting from potential profitability.

Since individuals have been separated from their substance in the public due to public policy and the debasing of value through fiat currencies, they can no longer compete with organized industries in the production of basic necessities, and therefore become voluntary servants thereof.

As per catch-22, individuals become increasingly dependent upon domestic and international corporations, not only for basic necessities, but also luxuries which they now can afford due to the efficiencies of mass-production and mass-marketing as corporations consume and consolidate independent commercial interests.

Corporations grow by leveraging mass-production and mass-marketing in a sort of politically correct Ponzi scheme. Because of their beneficial legal status, they have access to substance (means of production) to a degree which individuals no longer have. Individuals are constrained to *form* (fiat monies) as an intermediary between themselves and the products of *substance* which the corporations provide.

Individuals must work increasingly harder and longer in order to maintain the levels of consumerism to which they have become accustomed, thereby increasing their dependence on and servitude to corporations in order to make up for the diminishing value of the fiat currencies upon which they are *dependent* for value.

Corporations exist for the manifest purpose of earning profits whether by leveraging assets or by reducing costs. Just as fiat monies are "mined" of their value through inflation (hidden taxation) and interest, commodities also have potential for being "diluted," "synthesized," and "genericized." Thus, durable goods tend to become less durable and foods less nutritious, e.g., plastics replace metals, monoculture crops replace genetically diversified organic foods.

Large corporations are more easily regulated than the mass of individuals, and revenue is more easily procured as the funneling affect channels increasing revenue through the large corporations. It is therefore in the best interests of both governments and corporations to be in "bed" together and promote corporate dominion throughout the world where *value* can be controlled more efficaciously through *voluntary* servitude, deflation of substance, and inflation of fiat monies.

In sum, we beat a path to the corporations because mass-production and leveraging enables cheaper goods. We seek cheaper goods since money is "tight," and money is tight because of loss of substance in the public and the continuous manipulation of the value of fiat currencies through inflation (hidden tax) and interest. We flock to corporations because of our loss of *individual* Power. Corporations exist for maximum profit, not for the Good of the individual, i.e., quasi-public corporations are all about manifest commercial Power *over.*

Commerce

As the most fundamental expression of the motive of control, commerce *is* ostensibly the basis for law and government as humans have ostensibly been exchanging goods and services long before the beginning of recorded history. Many of the earliest written symbols were used for accounting. Indeed, a more archaic definition of commerce is—sexual *intercourse.*

Since the *sexual paradigm of Power* is the basis of all other forms of Power, the political and supernatural paradigms are analogous to sexual reproduction, e.g., acquisition of a resource (mate), controlling of a resource (pregnancy), synthesizing of the resource (development of fetus), and finally, potentiality in a new source of energy or means of production (offspring).

It probably wasn't long before the first symbol-using animals realized that you can't have too much of a Good thing, or *anything* of value, for that matter. While it is *Good* to own a silo of grain, man does not live by bread alone, where a surplus of value can always be traded for *other* commodities of value.

Once it was discovered that a surplus commodity could be traded for other Goods and services, it likely wasn't long before humans began accumulating plentiful commodities in hopes of exchanging them for items which were rarer and more difficult to obtain, thus outcompeting other wholesalers through "specialization." A "final" step in basic commerce would have been the art of leveraging of commodities, i.e., "value" through buying low and selling high.

One such strategy would have been to procure something locally and cheaply which was rare and/or valuable to a distant buyer and deliver to it them, hence the ancient form of commerce known as "shipping." To be able to "float" large quantities of commodities with relatively minimal human effort and expense to nearly unlimited distant markets would certainly have been a major step in the consolidation of Power in the form of economic control through technology.

Another strategy of buying low and selling high is the art of manufacturing, i.e., taking relatively cheap and raw materials and creating more sophisticated items of utility and convenience for sale at a higher cost.

A third major form of buying low and selling high is trading value for interest, i.e., dealing in values of exchange, e.g., historically in Europe, the goldsmiths were adept at safekeeping an individual's accumulated value, typically in the form of gold or silver, and recasting it into coinage or objects of art for a fee.

However, they soon discovered that it was more convenient for customers to exchange the receipts they acquired in lieu of their precious metals as it was more risky and cumbersome to physically carry said metals upon one's person.

Since fewer and fewer depositors actually reclaimed their gold and silver (as depositors began to exchange receipts in lieu of metals), the goldsmiths discovered that they could issue additional receipts as loans with interest to new customers based upon the metals they held in reserve. Thus the beginnings of the fractional fiat banking system we know today.

The ancient art of shipping established the rules of international commerce, enabling city-states to rise and dominate, thereby enabling the development of manufacturing which culminated in the Industrial Revolution.

As a shipper, one can purchase or build additional or more efficient ships, thereby leveraging one's means of production, however, new ships have *substantive*, fixed costs. In manufacturing, one can produce cheaply made items or devise more efficient methods of manufacturing, yet again, such items have fixed, substantive costs and must compete against items of a similar nature.

However, a purely *symbolic* form of value (as per a hollow signifier) can be manipulated in innumerable ways. If one can *claim* to be in possession of value and in fact is *believed* to be (Axiom 11), and therefore makes an offer to a second party to lend said "value" upon agreement to the terms of a contract and the second party agrees, it creates a contract based upon trust (*form*), rather than *substance*.

Thus, whether or not *there ever was* sufficient (substantive) value on deposit in the form of gold, silver, or other substance becomes irrelevant. As long as all agreed debts and credits balance out in the end and the "shell game" is played astutely, it is possible to create value out of appearances alone, as per the *Wonderful Wizard of Oz* (*Oz* being the official unit of measurement of precious metals).

The exchange of goods and services is based on the motives of the *individual* Good, *not* the (Good) of the collective. Flowering plants produce seductive blossoms of color, scent, and nectar in order to seduce pollinators for the manifest purpose of their own survival. The flower itself becomes a latent vessel of reproduction in its manifest function of providing nourishment to its pollinator.

Within the sexual paradigm, intercourse is pursued not for the manifest Good of the partner nor the community, but the gratification of the *individual*. The process of acquiring a mate and soliciting intercourse does not entail an egalitarian group effort wherein each suitor participates equally in the acquisition of every other suitor's mate, nor does it include equal mating rights. Quite the opposite is apparent in nature as ravenous competition ensues between suitors.

As symbol-using animals, we must promote the *illusion* of manifest Good, i.e., that "all men are created equal" in all of our motives, such that competition for mating and sexual rites are obscured within a matrix of meanings and counter-meanings, e.g., what it means to: date, properly socially interact, conform to acceptable gender roles, be socioeconomically suitable, have proper beliefs, have proper contexts of behavior, etc.

However, just below the surface of such idealized (Good) conditions, we are ravenous and self-centered in our mating and procreation practices as they form the basis of Power within our political paradigm of Power *over*.

All other motives are likewise manifestly driven by the *individual* and individual interests as opposed to a collective Good. This is not to suggest that it is impossible for social *collective* actions to be manifestly for the *ostensible* Good of the community, nor that an individual may decide to manifestly share food, sex, shelter, and resources as equally as possible, but rather that it is the nature of humans to satiate the *self* as the manifest motive of being. Once the self is satiated, many latent functions of "Good" occur in nature and in society, i.e., survival of the species, charity, etc.

Language-caused guilt motivates us to pursue all manner of manifestly "Good" social actions for the latent effect of rising in the hierarchy, but only as a guilty reflex in our natural, manifest pursuit of individual Goodness.

As producers of commodities, we are equally motivated by individual gain through organized effort. Our dominant motive in commerce is *control* through maximum profits. Corporations promote the illusion of a manifest motive of public "Good" through advertising and massive PR campaigns.

The false storefronts of the old American West are iconic of such campaigns as they were constructed so as to make a place of business appear larger and more successful (Axiom 9). Such *formal* illusions are ubiquitous throughout commerce, e.g., sexual suitors manifest their most favorable qualities and attributes when dating, just as product packaging and marketing accentuates any benefits and qualities of products while de-accentuating any negative latent effects or patent fallacies.

A consummate exemplar of the orientation of self-interest on both the consumption and production sides of commerce is found in the blind clamor for consumption on behalf of contemporary consumers and indiscriminate fervor in production on behalf of producers who once produced implements of war used against the consumer's country of origin.

From the sexual through the supernatural paradigms of Power, commerce is manifestly driven by individual motives (needs) of empowerment within nature and society, and although there is much latent "Good" therein, commerce, as a motive of control, is manifestly driven by our manifest will to Power *over.*

Money

As the symbolic lifeblood of the motive of control money is the epicenter of symbolic evolution and Power. "Legal" tender (color of money) is now an entirely symbolic form of wealth, where an individual holding a few stacks of paper or electronic digits on a computer (money of account) server may be considered much wealthier than an individual holding real estate or property of substance (money of exchange).

Historically, money, as a symbolic medium of value, has been linked to rarity and substance such as precious metals. Purely *symbolic* money can be manipulated through inflation and deflation, and if detached from the value of *substance,* becomes *lawfully* worthless, giving those in authority a "blank check" to create and control value out of *nothing.*

In the United States for example, the dollar has been inflated at a rate of 2,285 percent from 1913 to 2015. A dollar at the time of this writing will purchase approximately what five cents would have in 1913 (the year the Federal Reserve was created on Jekyll Island off the coast of Georgia by a conglomerate of *private* financiers).

Throughout history, rulers and profiteers have sought to extract tribute and wealth from the masses through deception, intimidation, taxation, and domination, more recently tribute has been extracted under the auspice of the greater "Good" of the masses, however an uncommon sense approach to modern money mechanics reveals an astutely played shell game designed to separate the masses from wealth of *substance.*

The international financiers were shrewd enough to recapture the Revolutionary War debt of the United States *of America* in 1789 following the aftermath of the French Revolutionary War (on behalf of King George III) so as to become the creditors of the soon-to-be *corporate* (privately-owned) *United States* under the US Constitution. With each subsequent seventy-year cycle of bankruptcy, the international financiers have demanded ever more surety, e.g., first from the bankrupt central government (1789) through the incorporation of the *United States*, next from the several states (1859) in the loss of sovereignty, next, the people (1929) in the loss of *substance* in the public, and most recently, the loss of *private* rights of the people in the public (democracy), post-1999.

If money is in fact the lifeblood of commerce, and commerce *is* the basis of symbolic Power, we should not be surprised to discover historical clusters of related events surrounding significant historical economic events, e.g., default on the American Revolutionary War debt, Shay's Rebellion, War of 1812 (central bank charter), American Civil War, WWII, the New Deal, JFK, 9/11, etc.

Since the US dollar *is* (currently) the world's reserve currency, and since the United States fought for its sovereignty thereby placing itself in fiduciary jeopardy (along with France), it is the most significant locus of study in terms of the motive of control through *economics*, however, most currencies today operate under similar monetary policy wherein fiat monies are issued as *debt* and inflated and manipulated as a latent form of *tribute*.

In the United States, *substance* was effectively replaced with *form* in 1933 as the people became bankrupt to the states under *House Joint Resolution 192*, generally accepted accounting practices *(GAAP)*, and *Publication 1212*, under the *New Deal*. Under this new policy, the people no longer have substance and therefore can no longer pay off debt, instead money is issued *as debt* which is created by the corporate "PERSON," i.e., "Authorized Representative," and "offset" with "credits." Therefore, every dollar of debt created (by *formal* agreement) is issued as a Federal Reserve *note,* i.e., promise to repay at some future point in time.

A bill represents a past debt, a note is issued for a current debt, and a bond is a promise to pay at a future point in time. US dollars are notes, i.e., current debts incurred by the use of the fiat money. The bond numbers thereupon match the bond numbers issued on birth certificates and SS cards, therefore US dollars are "bonded" by the life energies of the masses who apply for benefits from the bankrupt state.

Essentially, the entire *world* has become bankrupted to the international financiers in a similar fashion through the issuance of fiat currencies as debt. Each unit of money issued represents the value it is issued for, *but does not include the interest due and payable for its issuance*, therefore it is mathematically *impossible* to pay off accruing debt with current monies (M1). New debt must be issued–at interest–to pay off old interest, etc.

Throughout history, men have attempted to control the issuance and value of money as the quickest route to economic control (Power). After the age of Enlightenment, as commerce and trade began to expand in Europe, a few enterprising entrepreneurs established the fiat banking system that is now ubiquitous throughout the world through the development of fractional reserve banking. Those private families now control world finances through the International Monetary Fund, the Bank for International Settlements, the Council on Foreign Relations, the Federal Reserve (US), the secretary of state, the secretary of treasury, and US monetary policy.

We analyze money subsequent to commerce as an economic motive of *control* here since commerce predates money in the evolution of Power, however, from a hierarchical perspective, money as a symbol competes with all other symbolic meaning as the *dominant* form of Power (as a God term), i.e., "Money *is* God" (Kenneth Burke).

Money represents Power for those who are authorized to issue and control its value *and* for those who use it to leverage value for profit, e.g., corporations. Contemporary money *is* debt plus interest, as such it represents a game of musical chairs, or hot potato, in which the ones ultimately owning debt get burned, while those who "leverage" it are empowered.

Those who issue the money risk nothing since they are already empowered to create value out of nothing *and* to control it. Those who utilize debt (leverage) in order to amass profits are empowered within a bankrupt world since they have more capacity to exchange "profits" for private substance (such as real estate or other means of production).

Those who leverage money (debt) become liberated from the physical servitude of "catching and tossing hot potatoes" since they are merely manipulating symbols, i.e., negative versus positive digits, while the dead corporate laborers bear the ultimate burden of risk and voluntary servitude.

Those who get burned are those who, at the end of the day, "own" or hold the balance of debt. These include the *state created* corporate PERSONS with whom the private individual *voluntarily* identifies him or herself as the responsible agent, i.e., as the *owners* of public debt in the form of mortgages, loans, consumer debt, and credit.

Many of these falsely believe themselves to be quasi-entrepreneurial due to their competitive salaries with benefits, however, unlike for-profit corporations, they are: fully liable in the public for claims and debts against them, constrained to some form of servitude in return for compensation, typically nonprofit-oriented therefore debt tends to equal "income," and typically do not invest in real property for the production of real (substantive) value outside of *debt*.

While for-profit corporations are amassing profits for the manifest purpose of Power through economic control, i.e., *ensuring themselves a chair* when the music stops and to have surplus credit, i.e., profits so that *they are not left holding the hot potato.* Corporate *citizens* are *accruing* debt such that when the music stops, someone *inevitably* loses, since mathematically, there aren't enough potatoes in circulation at any given point in time to pay both principal *and* interest, and since there simply is more debt (hot potatoes) than assets distributed amongst the masses.

Before the loss of substance in the public in 1933 in the United States, many families owned farms and worked the land and/or had family-owned local businesses with relatively minimal debt. Many people were skilled artisans and craftsmen who could construct their own homes and manage their own assets.

Today, the vast majority of citizens are merely *tenants on the land* clustered together near corporate centers of production and utterly dependent upon corporate and municipal services for nearly all quotidian needs. Small, family-owned businesses are absorbed or annihilated by mega-corporate interests in order to eliminate competition and maximize profits as people become increasingly dependent upon money (debt) and credit in order to survive.

We might expect to observe such trends if in fact the substantive value of the people and commodities were replaced by fiat currencies which were mandated as "legal tender" with a current inflation rate of 2,285.9 percent, and subject to taxes and fees.

In sum, if this brief analysis of money, as a motive of control, were a comprehensive treatise of fact rather than *the subjective standpoint of this writer*, it should be worthy of several books of *uncommon-sense* analysis and cross-reference. Even so, we may have *digressed* into appearing to put forth statements of *fact* through specificity of dates and entities, etc., however, such an abridged overview represents a mere pittance of *interrelated* data which is readily available (in such postmodern times) to the uncommon critical thinker.

If money (as we know it) *is* the lifeblood of commerce, and commerce is the basis of all human interaction, and all human meaning is mediated though symbols, and money is nothing *if not a symbol*, then *it is highly significant* to analyze as a motive in our search for human purpose.

Money (as we know it) could not exist for the *manifest* moral Good of humanity or it wouldn't bear excessive cost in interest, taxes, or fees and would be used only as an efficient medium in the equitable exchange of goods and services. Generally accepted accounting practices alone implies the motive of Power *over*, e.g., the *legal* (as opposed to lawful) right of some to create value *out of nothing*, and *charge others for the privilege*.

Resources

Non-symbol using creatures live in balance with the environments which gave rise to them. Natural resources are the basis of empowerment in nature, i.e., as per the sexual paradigm. Within the political paradigm, whatever *natural* conditions gave rise to and sustained humans are no longer tenable since we have become "separated from our natural conditions by instruments of our own making" (Burke) & (Axiom 21).

In the political, as in the sexual paradigm, the most essential economic resource is that of a sexual mate or mates as the method of reproduction of individuals, without whom *human* economic activity is not possible. Pre-symbolic economics involves successful sexual reproduction through physical domination and access to and control of resources. Within the political paradigm, resources are defined and managed symbolically, not only in relation to what constitutes a "mate" and the contexts under which a mate may or may not be acquired, but what constitutes a "resource" and the contexts within which it may or may not be acquired.

Kenneth Burke's actus/status pair is elucidative herein in that organized *acts,* over time, become institutionalized *statuses,* e.g., a familial hunter-gatherer tribe in the act of hunting and gathering may stumble upon a favorable geographic region with plentiful resources, thereby negating the need for a nomadic existence.

As a tribe settles in a region, a new status arises including a need for *control* over their new territory—i.e., as per Maslow's "security"— against competing tribes, therefore defensive armaments and guards are put in place; and what was formerly a region of hunter-gatherer *act*ivity (the *act* of hunting-gathering) becomes a *state* of organized existence where former acts of hunting and gathering are no longer tenable.

The symbolic re-creation of "reality" above, the sexual paradigm effectively "fixes" individuals hierarchically within the political paradigm (Appendix III). Where individuals are born—*who* their parents are, their *occupations*, and the *assets* they control, etc., all add up to a particular social *status* within the political paradigm wherein one's *status* is contained in one's *acts* and one *acts* according to one's *status*.

Although we retain a posteriori instincts outside of symbolic meaning, they are effectively renegotiated within the grid of political meaning. We may instinctively be attracted to a member of the opposite sex as a function of the status of our natural sexuality, however, as Powerful as such emotions may be, they are overpowered by a veritable plethora of political filters of *status*. This is not to suggest that it is *impossible* to mate outside of socioeconomic, cultural, or racial statuses, or to consciously resist the status quo, but that such acts implicate a risk of social status on behalf of one party or the other within the net hierarchy of the political paradigm.

Status and interhuman relationships have an intimate relationship. Within the symbolic (and non-symbolic) world, everything begins with status, e.g., whatever acts one is capable of are dependent upon one's status. The more expertise one has across diverse disciplines, the more value one has and a correspondingly larger network within the hierarchy.

Inasmuch as we are *symbolically* interdependent, beneficial exchange of service and ideas is by definition the "source" in our subheading above, "Re*sources,*" i.e., the pool of shared symbolic skill and knowledge into which we dip in order to survive.

"Resourcefulness" can represent the quality of an individual in terms of ability to efficiently utilize time and materials independent of others, however, the ability to *have* time and materials and knowledge to use them is a function of social interaction and technology through *communication*. Knowledge of technique, with respect to surviving in the wilderness or constructing a shelter, is obtained through symbolic language through social interaction as a function of social *status*.

An individual is not necessarily "fixed" to his or her social status at birth, since an individual tends to grow and develop. As an individual ages, social status changes correspondingly, however, like fish suspended in water (Axiom 12), we are born into a cultural status of which we are unaware (at least in the lower castes), such that by the time we *become* aware, cultural values and beliefs, i.e., "reality," has become entrenched so as to have us relatively "fixed" within the hierarchical matrix.

Although there may in fact be instances of rags to riches, and obscurity to fame, no one is an island (Axiom 17), therefore some form of social resource can always be shown to be an *actus* in the creation of *status*.

Assets and money are merely *symbols* of status. One does not accumulate them in the absence of status. An individual of *low* social status may inherit or win significant assets, but any shift in social status is limited and dubious. One who wins a lottery for example will gain status in financial circles as long as they can *control* their wealth and thus gain in economic status, however social status is a complex function of a confluence of acts (actions), not merely wealth.

Status is a function of wealth, education, social service, trustworthiness, etc. The higher one's social status, the higher one is scrutinized. It would be difficult for a lottery winner or beneficiary to achieve equivalent social status to that of a doctor or CEO of equal wealth (in the absence of pre-existing equivalent status).

In the United States, as in other parts of the world, natural resources were once there for the taking, one merely needed to file a claim and work it in order to achieve the benefits of economic control by exploitation resources. Those who did (Axioms 29 and 30) undoubtedly did so due to *some* prior knowledge or mentorship (social resource), and in doing so, seized upon a great opportunity in leveraging of status (Axiom 29 and 30).Many acts in the composition of status were implicated therein, i.e., industriousness, resourcefulness, entrepreneurship, responsibility, dedication, self-respect, self-confidence, etc.

Historically, natural resources were so significant to humans as to be conflated with the Gods. Today, natural resources are for the greater part *legally* restricted (due to bankruptcy of the people and their loss of substance and private rights in the public) except through petition, i.e., paying tribute to the state in the form of *fiat monies*. Money of *account* (not of *exchange*) has become *God*, since it is the medium through which resources may be "legally" obtained.

Those who *ultimately* control natural resources are those who are authorized to issue and control the symbolic forms of legal value through which all natural resources must be traded. Money therefore *is* the universal resource, that is to say, *debt* (as form) is the universal resource which replaces *substantive* natural resources of the land.

Those individuals and families who were fortunate and industrious enough to seize the day, file claims, and develop natural resources, today govern the upper echelons of the Pyramid of Power together with those who have seized *financial* control.

The only resources remaining for individuals in the lower echelons of society are their own lives' energies and (*formal*) "credits" issued in the form of *debt* as a function of an individual's economic status *within* the political paradigm.

Since we merely accept reality as it is presented to us (Axiom 12), we clamor over one another as we compete for increasing indebtedness (in the form of fiat monies) as the only "legal" resource redeemable for *substantive* natural (and technological) resources. Our lives' energies drain away (as a water bucket full of holes) through inflation and overtaxed currency (debt).

The motive of control manifest in the hierarchical distribution of resources has ostensibly at no time been about manifest moral "*Good*." The resource of a sexual mate in the sexual paradigm has consistently been a source of contention and competition through dominance in nature. Competition over food and other resources is likewise observed in nature.

If the manifest motive of moral "Good" was the dominant motive in the distribution of resources within the political (symbolic) paradigm, all would be shared equally, i.e., mates, social status, natural resources, money, etc. The political paradigm is *manifestly* about leveraging Power *over* through the control and redistribution of *resources*, i.e who gets what.

Consubstantiation (Love and Belonging)

Sexuality

Within the political paradigm, the sex drive of the sexual paradigm becomes meaningful and therefore political. What is considered acceptable or unacceptable is regulated through cultural narratives (folkways, mores) of "Good" versus evil" (action), and one's social status is *significantly* influenced by one's sexual status since sexual conquest, reproduction, and alliance is of *primary social significance.*

A young, uncommitted, sexually active individual is highly significant to others of a similar demographic within his or her sphere of social influence as direct competition in pursuit of a mate or mates as well as a potential mate themselves. Such an individual is highly significant to the parents of prospective mates and vice versa since familial membership is the most fundamental unit of political and social Power. Likewise, siblings and extended relatives are implicated by the social status of any potential suitor (Axioms 4, 17, and 20) as is she by them.

In terms of society at large, a young, unattached, sexually active individual (particularly heterosexual male) is typically deemed to be *less* economically stable, dependable, and satisfied than an individual in a long-term, committed relationship (see Émile Durkheim). Such an individual *tends* to be less socially connected due to his or her uncommitted and therefore socially transient status.

Sex and sexual reproduction (as opposed to asexual reproduction) is an evolutionary development which arose due to certain ostensible advantages of genetic diversity and reproductive specialization. Heterosexual intercourse is the *most fundamental* and *natural* property of all sexually reproductive beings. Successful sexual reproduction in nature is a function of genetic dominance. This is not to suggest that there is some fundamental moral Good in the universe which determines dominance or success, but rather, that whatever random genetic traits best match random conditions of context survive as dominant (a vastly superior genetic mutation *may* have once arisen but gone extinct due merely to poor timing and/or context).

Within the political paradigm, where meaning is *subjective* and sex *is the most fundamental* component of human Power, the meaning of human sexuality is perhaps the most contested and controversial of any meaning (other than the meaning of meaning itself) within the political paradigm. There could not exist technological control over others (as per the political paradigm) on a grand scale if individual alpha males continued to dominate local populations of females, thereby assuring the status quo of the evolutionary sexual paradigm. Language and technology have allowed for the development of the self, the ego, and awareness of Power as a function of the symbolic.

Many beliefs, rituals, and practices have arisen over thousands of years with respect to human nature and sexuality in opposition to the natural brutish condition of the sexual paradigm, i.e., one of the more fundamental and profound narratives of Western cultures is the Christian narrative of the *fall of man.*

The creation narrative places the origin and nature of human kind within the motive of "Good". The Garden of Eden represents an exalted state of "Goodness", i.e., Godliness, wherein man is corrupted (corruptible) by the forces of "evil," i.e., nature. The "fall of man," which is precipitated by his corruptibility, implicates human beings as double-minded as represented by the division between man and God and by sexual opposition. Duality and opposition represent evil as symbolic of a separation from the unity of Truth and the singularity of God (Good).

In the creation narrative, the differential sexual attributes of Adam and Eve, i.e., genitalia, represent division and opposition to the singularity of spirit and being represented in God. Adam and Eve therefore are ashamed to expose their corrupt and divisive natures in the presence of God.

Rather than existing eternally as immortal beings in the singular presence of God, Adam and Eve become mortal beings who conceive and bear fruit through the divisiveness of the flesh. Thus the origin of guilt, shame, and embarrassment in human sexuality arises from our fundamental corruptible human nature.

However, double-mindedness and contradiction ostensibly arises throughout such narratives (since language and meaning are subjective in nature) where God *commands* Adam and Eve to "go forth and be fruitful and multiply" as corrupted beings of the flesh, as less than Godly, *in sin*.

If differences in sexuality in nature are related to provoking the sex drive, i.e., pheromones, physical features, audio stimuli, etc., *and* they are likewise related to sexual provocation in symbol-abusing animals, i.e., humans, and it is desirable to control the sexual and therefore reproductive behavior of humans within an ordered and hierarchical society, then it would naturally follow that sexual stimuli, i.e., nakedness, and intimate behavior must be controlled as a primary condition of an ordered society.

Who gets whom under which conditions in a hierarchical society must be determined through a system of symbolic entitlement rather than brute force alone. Therefore, such purely animalistic drives of the sexual paradigm must be subdued in service of the "Good" of the hierarchical social structure. In such a system, unrestricted sexuality becomes taboo, thereby instilling a social sense of guilt, shame, and embarrassment in the public (Axioms 14 and 20).

According to the standpoint of this writer, there doesn't appear to be *any* significant argument for sexuality being based in a manifest moral motive of "Good." From a creationist's perspective, sexuality (duality) *is* ostensibly a condition and sign *of* moral decay, while from an evolutionary perspective, it is the primary basis for profound contention and competition within species. Beyond mere survival and homeostasis, sexuality *is* the motivational epicenter in the struggle for Power *over*.

Gender

There are essentially two gender types of which this writer is aware from which all others appear to appropriate characteristics: masculine and the feminine, based upon the female and male sexes. In evolution, the sexes and sexual functions of living organisms are merely *inventions* of nature, not categories carved in stone. There are alternate types, e.g., asexual (as per cell division) and hermaphroditic (organisms which alternate between female and male).

Just as human genes retain our evolutionary heritage (as observable in the developmental stages of the human fetus) from single-cell organisms to Homo Sapiens, each sex, female and male, retains the sexual characteristics of the other. *If* evolution is driven by random mutation and adaptation, and *if* all (or nearly all) humans survive (due to technology and social mandate), and *if* we, humans, have altered our environments such that there is no longer any natural way of being in the world (Axioms 21 and 23), we should expect to observe a diversity of *genotypes* within our species and a resultant manifestation of divergent *phenotypes* (as compared with other species) inclusive of sexual characteristics, e.g., *if* androgenic and estrogenic hormones influence the development of male and female characteristics respectively, *and if* particular levels of both hormones occur naturally in *both* sexes, and *if* all individuals deemed to be heterosexual can be shown to have varying amounts of both hormones, male and female, *then* we should expect to observe mutations on the border between the traditional sexes resulting in greater fluctuations in the distribution of hormones and any resultant phenotypical traits, i.e., female versus male.

If from a creationist standpoint the sexes (female and male) are carved in stone, then we should not *expect* to observe any instances of genetic hormonal variability nor resultant phenotypical traits within the sexes. Ironically, even though both genotypical and phenotypical sexual traits *are* empirically observable among both sexes, and there is no fundamental connection between gender and sex, a creationist's viewpoint seems to *promote* gendered stereotypes *as sexuality*.

An evolutionary perspective does not discount the effects of social or cultural conditioning (Axioms 14, 20, and 21) with its innumerable contradictions in meaning and interpretation. The symbol-using and abusing (human) animal can *and does* alter its behavior *purposefully* according to innumerable *motives*, however, individuals are manifestly oriented toward the Good *of themselves*.

If an individual could be identified as genetically "normal" in terms of biological-sexual orientation but chooses homosexuality instead, there must be *some* perception of social injustice ("evil") suffered on behalf of the individual related to human or sexual relationships as a *motive* for *resistance* against the "norm" (Axiom 6) or some other form of social indoctrination which "purifies" the choice.

In such instances, it is not "unadulterated evil" which precipitates the choice but a confluence of *social* factors (Axiom 17), i.e., one could be raised from an infant to believe in a particular sexual orientation, or one could have been molested or abused by a "normal" member of the opposite sex. In such instances, the locus of "evil" would reside within the culture, *not* the individual.

Any choice other than heterosexuality *could* in fact be the result of some unadulterated evil "force," i.e., the "voice" of a demon, or the voice of a demon working through an agent, or any similar motive, such as the impetus to suddenly drive one's automobile over a cliff. Under such circumstances, "evil" must be some force *over* individual will, since humans do not act except out of some *motive* of perceived manifest or latent Good (benefit) attributable to the self (Axioms 6 and 28).

Gender, as the *culturally* symbolic progeny of sexuality, does not appear to be oriented in the manifest motive of moral "Goodness," particularly if it emerges from the *scourge of sexuality* as a result of *original sin*. Rather, manifestation of gender arises as a socio-political response in the symbolic struggle over meaning within the primal and highly contested paradigm of sexuality, i.e., a manifest motive of Power *over* identity within the political paradigm.

Socio-Sexual Economics

If we consider economics as encompassing the production, consumption, and transfer of wealth, and wealth as an abundance of value, then socio-sexual economics is about the production and consumption of social value.

Ultimately, all value *is* social value. Resources, money, and commerce are merely signs and symbols of the social economy which gives rise to them. Social value is founded upon an individual's *perceived* Power in relation to subjectivity within the Pyramid of Power (Axioms 1 and 3).

Social economics is analogous to hierarchy within our PoP. She/he who is perceived as more susceptible to subjectivities achieves a relatively lower social status in our PoP, while she/he who is perceived as more dominant attains a higher status.

The epicenter of the *social* economy is the *sexual* economy driven by natural desire, attraction, and communication, as its primary motives. Although driven by the primal motive of desire, the sexual economy is also motivated by the practical and hierarchical economics of the greater social economy, thus "portliness" *may* become a culturally *attractive* feature of a prospective mate as a *cultural* sign of "abundance," and thus *aesthetics* of attraction are to some degree, subjective and culturally relevant.

Within the sexual paradigm, desire and attraction are ostensibly driven by various manifestations of *fitness* which are hardwired within the brain. If we were to analyze who is deemed "attractive" through contemporary images in art, media, and public opinion, we would discover that beauty is a function of both physical *fitness* and incredibly *average* physical and psychological proportionality (Axiom 28). Physical attributes which are advantageous in successful reproduction are desirable by nature.

Those who are generally considered "attractive" represent a *median* range of *possible* attributes, i.e., not too portly, not too lean, not too tall, nor too short, average facial features, not too brash nor too meek, etc. Average in nature is the balance between extremes in *random mutation*, i.e., the archetypical epicenter as the representative ideal of a species. Thus, sexual aesthetics, i.e., beauty, is consistent with Truth in the Goodness of nature (Appendix V).

Attractiveness thus is a major factor of sexual and social economics. Aesthetics of attraction are not only influenced by naturally hardwired biological instincts, but also by socially constructed ideals. Attractive and sexually appealing individuals not only have Power within the sexual economy, but also in the social economy at large as universal *symbols* of desirability and success.

From the (Western) cultural perspective of this writer, it is the "average" *female* body by far which is adorned and exalted as a cultural *idol*. That is not to suggest *any* female body, per se, but specifically the female body "*in flower*," i.e., within the *sexually productive* years. Women's fashions are ostensibly designed to accentuate (display) the female body—hair is typically worn long as symbolic of the more *natural* aesthetic state of women, and jewelry is utilized as further adornment, as per religious idols.

Although some feminists might prefer to "reclaim" the female body from objective "exploitation" and "degradation," *and* although "beauty is only skin deep" and "you can't judge a book by its cover" *and* women could just as easily choose to resist traditional gender roles, a majority of women would ostensibly choose to conform, since there is *Power* in the sexual economy.

The socio-sexual economy *is* culture. Through innumerable channels of communication, the "incredibly average" become aware of their socio-sexual status early on, thereby becoming inculcated. As Western society moves away from production and agrarianism toward information and consumerism, we might expect to see an exponential rise in the sexual economy with the idolized female body at its cultural epicenter.

Perhaps the best example of the cult of the *feminine sex idol* is to be experienced at a local shopping mall where everywhere is found the cult of beauty and the female sex idol. One may observe the cultural influence of the female sex idol in the female patrons therein who consume and display the products of beauty and femininity, i.e., clothing, jewelry, makeup, etc., even amongst those not yet "in flower," as well as those beyond.

Sex and the sex drive are so primal and ubiquitous to humans that as we abandon the plow to the field and the pots and pans to the kitchen and direct our attention toward media and it toward us, our basic drives and desires are brought to the surface as though from Pandora's box as we become a culture of the spectacle (see "Society of the Spectacle" by Guy Debord). The once manifest *underground* torrent of "pornography" becomes latent, mainstream sexual innuendo.

Women *could* resist denigration of equality, intellectualism, pride, etc. by *resisting* cultural stereotypes of beauty and sexuality, yet it appears the majority manifestly choose not to, since human nature is eesentially animnal nature based in an inherent biological sexual economy. Media and advertising is saturated with images of the female sex idol indicating a profound cultural bias for sexual desirability, while reifying ideal gendered stereotypes.

In nature, male empowerment is based on dominance and competitiveness. Female empowerment is based on successful sexual reproduction through successful attraction of a dominant male. *Evolutionarily* speaking, the female's Power is based on attractiveness and fitness in raising offspring, *thus* it is not counterintuitive if a majority of females appear to be *manifestly* motivated toward attractiveness in sexuality.

Truth *may* be equal to morality and morality equal to equality. However, if Truth is equal to beauty and beauty consists of sexual attractiveness, then there can be no morality in beauty since sexual attractiveness is not *equal* in males nor females; *and* in females, is analogous to male competitiveness in pursuit of dominance. Female "sex idols" *compete* with one another directly for ideal mates within the sexual economy and within the larger social economy as socially symbolic "ideals," thereby stimulating commerce through performance and cultivation of the sexual economy.

Although conception is the object of the sexual economy in nature, success is dependent upon physical dominance and assertiveness particularly on the part of the male. Within the political paradigm of symbolic meaning, there are a veritable plethora of subjective meanings which also must be negotiated before successful conception can occur (outside of rape), most of which are virtually subjective and culturally understood.

The term "dating" is *culturally* understood to mean: intentionally associating with specified members of the opposite sex for the manifest purpose of potential sexually related intimacy. Thus the term *dating* from an etymological perspective comes to mean soliciting sexual intimacy in a socially understood and acceptable manner, as opposed to setting a date for some specified activity at some point in time with or without another individual.

Even if we understand the above definition of dating, it gives us no clue as to any correct or incorrect behaviors and actions implicated within the term or definition. An individual who was not properly cultured within the term would not know—*how* to dress, *if* to dress, *how* to speak, *if* to speak, of *what* to speak, *which* mannerisms to express, *which* to suppress, *how* to organize details, *if* to organize details, and to *what* extent. As if these subjectivities were not enough within symbolic meaning (Axiom 14), there is a missing term as a *prerequisite* to "dating" i.e., how does one move from a state of "non-dating" to a state of "dating," and *how* does one know when they have arrived?

Thus the entire socio-sexual economic paradigm is dependent upon culturally understood subjective meanings. Unlike in nature where the individual is stimulated to seek a mate and to copulate and reproduce, in the symbolic world, the individual must negotiate the scattered winds of contradictory cultural meanings where on one extreme, an individual's social status and quality of life is utterly *founded* upon success within the socio-sexual economy, and on the other, sex and sexuality are culturally sublimated or disparaged as human conditions or topics which are *taboo*.

A particular cultural myth may enculturate one to believe that obtaining a sexual mate is *not* a social endeavor but rather a function of supernatural forces, i.e., "There is someone for everyone," or, "God provides." Even though it can be reasonably demonstrated that successful pairings are merely a function of *attraction, proximity, similarity* and *communication*.

One must first experience desire *and* be *attracted* to the object of one's desire, also, one must be *proximitous* to the object of one's desire since *intimacy* is antithetical to *separation* (Axiom 3 and 17), and one must have similarity of *interest* (Axiom 26). And of course, there are no meaningful relationships outside of communication. Such empirical properties are observable as prerequisites to nearly all social relations.

Within the political paradigm, subjective meaning is scattered about like bread crumbs left to the whims of contradictory cultural forces (Axiom 3). Public education systems are more concerned with a compliant and docile workforce than sovereign, liberally educated individuals and promote an educational agenda pursuant to their interests (Axiom 14). The socio-sexual economy is dominated by the successful (Axioms 8 and 9) who are empowered literally and culturally through knowledge and a culturally inherited sense of entitlement.

Sexual reproduction is at the epicenter of the socio-sexual economy as the most natural and fundamental basis of Power through regeneration. Thus, the choice to have children is the most fundamental political motive within our political paradigm.

Within symbolic language, we can reconstruct meaning in any manner we desire, however, *if* human individuals are significant and arise due to sexual activity, then it is the Power to *choose* and *ability* to engage in sexual activity which is the precursor to creating individuals.

It is reasonable to assume that *most* human conceptions are a result of persons engaged in co-constructing reality through the process of giving "voice" to particular culturally prescribed activities, e.g., "dating," attending a soiree, etc. which are prerequisite to greater intimacy. Knowledge of the mechanics of conception as prerequisite to human creation is a socially constructed reality beyond nature, and thus knowledge of conception is implicated in human choice.

If it is true that within our symbolic matrix of meaning there are no "accidents," but rather *confluences of choices in action* (some beyond our control), then we should expect to experience limited need for abortion. The subjective line of meaning which separates the sexes is subservient to *choice*, i.e., of responsibility, of association, of context, etc.

If each individual from fertilized egg, to decrepit popper, were valued at $1 million—progressively remunerable to the responsible parties as long as the individual remained alive—one wonders how prevalent abortion would be as a consequence of choice within the socio-sexual economy.

If the submotive of *consubstantiation*, i.e., *sexual intimacy*, was manifestly a motive of moral "Good," all individuals would be *equally* concerned with each other's intimate status. Even where a supernatural force is unknowingly blocking those who were morally corrupt from obtaining sexual intimacy, this should not in any way deter an *attempt* on behalf of others to ensure *equal* distribution of relational "status."

The motive of consubstantiation, i.e., the desire to share *substance* with others, i.e., belief (Axiom 11), and therefore, "reality" cannot be based in the motive of "moral" "Good," since belief, and therefore "reality," is not only differentiated due to subjective meaning *between* cultures, but between *individuals*.

The socio-sexual economy is driven by the primal evolutionary drive of sexual reproduction and is highly contested within the political paradigm as the most fundamental locus of manifest Power *over.*

Family

Any consubstantiation between humans constitutes some manifestation of Power (Axioms 17, 18, 19, and 20). Within the hierarchical social-sexual economy, consubstantiation between infants is the least socially significant, followed by non-heterosexuals, followed by "loner males" (unattached, adult beta males), followed by "unattached" beta females (typically not "loners" due to multilateral social interconnectivity), followed by heterosexual couples, and finally *the family* as the core political Power unit of society.

Consubstantiation entails all forms of shared belief therefore any combination of beliefs outside of "family values" *could* exercise a more Powerful voice politically as long as there were strength in numbers. However, if the counter-values included not having children, "family values" would ultimately dominate since successful sexual reproduction is prerequisite to the socio-sexual economy (assuming of course "family values" entail successful sexual reproduction). Although consubstantiation occurs across many dialectics, ultimately, it is *reproductive* consubstantiation which dominates politically, thus the social-sexual (political) hierarchy, i.e., the family, as most likely to produce offspring.

Amongst families, those who are more highly vested in resources reside higher in the political paradigm (Axioms 18 and 26). Sexual intimacy *is* the foundation upon which the family is constructed as a foundation for increasing potentiality in social consubstatiation, however, social dominance is a function of *symbolic domination*, i.e., knowledge of technique (Axiom 25).

Power begets Power (Axiom 9). As the "family" gains in political dominance due to its dominance within the sexual economy, values within the social economy become co-opted in favor of the family values, i.e., the family as the most politically correct and potent social unit deserving of the highest esteem in society.

The family also becomes a unit for political control similar to that of domestic livestock, inasmuch as the family is engineered as an easily managed economic unit whose purpose is to produce a compliant and docile labor force. A stark counter-example would be *manifest* slavery where economic interests vested in land and other means of production forcefully induce others of lower economic castes to perform menial and undesirable tasks as a basis of wealth and Power.

Within manifest slavery, not only are males and females selected for their favorable attributes as *laborers,* but by extension, as *breeding stock* for new laborers. Within manifest slavery, males and females need not be allowed to mingle and associate, but ostensibly are, thus creating a latent breeding program which ensures a compliant pool of laborers.

Within *latent* slavery, a similar model of social engineering occurs *structurally* such that the very structure of the society itself engineers compliant social roles and behaviors through dictums of rule and authority. Within such a latent structure, it is not necessary to forcefully induce compliance, but rather *engineer* compliance as the best possible course of social action, e.g., as per the *Wonderful Wizard of* (Oz). (Axiom 12).

Due to symbolic language, socioemotional aesthetics become implicated within the social-sexual economy. Animalistic aesthetics of desire and pleasure become meaningful and therefore *purposefully* pursued. "Love" becomes a moralized reconstruction of the *pleasure* of sexual intimacy. However, if moralistic love was the manifest motive for sexual intimacy as opposed to conditions of *proximity, similarity, attraction,* and *communication* all of humanity would act as one equal platonic family, regardless of sexual desire.

Since sexuality *is* implicated in intimacy, there is a bias toward love being directed toward objects of desire, as opposed to being shared platonically. This, in addition to biases in *similarities* and *proximities* which are exclusive of others, is indicative of the motive of manifest Power *over* all other morally prescribed relationships, thus undermining any fundamentally moralized concept of family values.

Marriage

Prior to the Enlightenment era and still to this day, the "sanctioning" of the sexual union of a couple was and is often overseen by a priest who bestows authority and condonation upon such carnal relationships, thereby sanctifying, authorizing, and elevating them to the higher social caste of the "blessed," thereby giving couples "voice" through ritualized elevation of social status and sanctified reproductivity.

Various manifestations of polygamy, i.e., polygyny, and to a much lesser extent, polyandry, have arisen due to ostensible religious and cultural dictums of "moral Good." However, cases of polygyny in particular appear to effectively replicate the common paradigm of sexual dominance from the sexual paradigm, i.e., that of a single male's dominance over several females. Whatever motive of moral "Good," manifest or latent, such constructions entail, they have the appearances of social dominance through *sexual dominance*, i.e., the most primal source of political Power.

All sexual relationships are by definition political in terms of who's getting whom. If platonic love were the manifest motive of sexual relationships, all would be shared equally, i.e., partners, intimacies, children, responsibilities, etc. Marriage therefore is a social-political contract formally recognizing who gets whom and by default, who doesn't.

If marriage is a social institution based in moral "Good," one wonders by what *mechanism* do couples come together, chose to marry, and have children, *exclusively*. A morally motivated pairing would consist of all assisting all in couplings equal to one's own, however, we would first need to dismantle subjectivity and the resultant social hierarchical economy so as to ensure all pairings were equal.

Within Western cultures, the bride is traditionally dressed in a long, flowing, white gown ostensibly symbolic of "purity" and the aesthetic flowing beauty of nature, as if to transpose the promiscuity and brutal competition of mating in nature into a morally sanctified rite of reproduction.

The groom typically is dressed in black (a traditional sign of Power), upper-class formal or business-like attire, is well-*groomed*, and therefore "civilized," respectable, and *socially serviceable*, i.e., his attire represents a utilitarian and formal social orientation as opposed to that of an autonomous self-serving bohemian.

The traditional marriage ritual occurs within a matrix of culturally significant meanings, all of which serve to reify the prescribed socioeconomic roles of the couple, i.e., clothes which are symbolic of expected social roles and attitudes, rings and diamonds as signs of exclusivity and ownership as well as economic value of the partner as an aesthetic object of attraction. The context reifies both a particular social-political sanctioning of the union as well as the couples solidarity therein.

The more highly ritualized the marriage ceremony, the more politically charged it becomes as a mechanism of moralizing and conferring of social status within the political paradigm. The contemporary marriage ceremony expropriates the central point of contention within the sexual paradigm (mating rites) and reifies it as socially sanctified and authorized. *Ritual* and *right* are closely related as in the social right to preferred status and reproduction within the culturally prescribed boundaries of status.

The state confers *status* upon married couples by offering economic and *legal* benefits due to the merger of its corporations which the couple represents as a breeding pair. In this manner, a marriage license represents another contractual indenturement to the state in return for benefits as per the birth certificate and SS card. By contrast, in a common law of the land marriage, a couple enters into a natural, lawful, and unencumbered agreement by *mutual consent* without need of deferring to political and or supernatural hierarchies of Power.

The paradigm of family is the microcosm of the socio-sexual economy out of which the political paradigm of Power arises. If marriage and "family values" were based upon the motive of manifest moral "Good," all resources and relationships would be shared equally. However, family, by nature, *is* exclusive, and therefore a manifest motive of Power *over*.

Community

The old French term, *comunité*, means to be reinforced by its source. As such, community represents the zenith of consubstantiation, since the community is the source of the individual. In terms of Maslow's need of "love and belonging" being "re-in-forced," i.e., empowered through common substance, is consummate with Burke's process of *identification*.

Community is the process of making things "common," and therefore "pure," through communication where "commonness" is the "substance" in consubstantiation. Once the "Good" of common ground is established and maintained (Axioms 17, 18, and 19), there is no limit to what *individuals* are capable of achieving.

Communication *is* the process of community through the establishment of predictability and continuity, i.e., the unity (oneness) of "comm-*unity.*" If the individual knows what to expect or not to expect within a community and such expectations remain relatively stable, the individual can then form new *unities* and technologies through communication, thereby *reinforcing* the original community or giving rise to new ones.

The predictability and continuity of the community likewise requires the individual to have some form of identity, or *role*, as a basis of interaction. This role could be merely as a "member" in need of basic support and emergency services or any combination of technological or social roles.

In order for an individual to assume a role, i.e., "identity," *someone* must *persuade* a second, or third, party or parties that in fact said individual is qualified to assume a particular identity or role, i.e., if the individual in question cannot communicate, someone *will* by default, assume the role of persuading others that the individual is either qualified, or not qualified, for a particular identity or role within the community (see *Nell*, the movie). In the above example, it is likely that this individual would be given the role of ward of the state.

As identities are established through roles, a community is maintained. However, established roles do not negate the need for communication, rather the need for communication increases in proportion to social complexity and specialization, i.e., technology with its specialized symbols (jargon).

The art of persuasion becomes *increasingly* complex and exigent in proportion to social complexity and technology. Although a community is constructed upon "common" relationships and meaning, a higher form of sense-making becomes exigent, i.e., an *uncommon* or *atypical* orientation to reasoning. Commonsense orientations include the taken-for-granted, the traditional, empirical observations, and generalizations, whereas an un-common-sense orientation includes, the questioning of everything, the permanence of change, the theoretical, and the specific.

In order to have predictability and continuity, an individual must acquire a community's system of knowing, i.e., *knowledge of technique* (knowledge of technique encompasses *all* human knowledge, i.e., humanities as well as the "hard" sciences, since *all* is knowledge and all is technique). The role, and therefore identity of the individual, must coincide with the technologies of a given community, e.g., its language.

Roles allow for social interaction within a community and at the same time establish a hierarchy of relationships, e.g., roles determine what acts (actions) are possible for the individual (who may have multiple roles), and actions determine status. An individual may study to become a doctor, and upon completion of a degree, decide *not* to practice and instead become a fry cook. Although she/he has the *formal* status of being a doctor due to her/his training, in *action*, her/his status, and therefore identity, becomes that of a fry cook.

Social hierarchy depends upon status, and status is determined by birth, community values, and culturally prescribed signs which are propagated by social institutions and the state, i.e., voice, activities, clothes, assets, social roles, etc.

What is *ultimately* "Good" for the community (society) is determined by the state, and that which the state will allow is determined by local community practices, e.g., a local community might have a basis in agriculture and therefore tend to be so biased in its latitude of acceptable roles. Conversely, another community may have a bias in adherence to religious practices and therefore be so biased.

Although many social experiments have been conducted wherein an egalitarian community cooperates collectively for the "Good" of its members, they tend to be few in number and tend not to endure. This writer is unaware of any fully egalitarian or democratic society devoid of some form of hierarchy.

Social stratification occurs due to the formation of in-groups and out-groups. Groups which are vested in a common interest (Axiom

26) which gives them more Power within a community become the dominant in-groups. Groups vested external to the dominant interests become the out-groups, just as less Powerful groups become the out-groupings of those groups.

In-groups and out-groups occur within all communities across *multiple* acts and statuses, e.g., "race" is a status implicated within historical and cultural significance. Inasmuch as there are signs and symbols attributable to a group, e.g., "racial," they become signs and symbols of relative status within a community.

Although from a scientific perspective all modern Homo Sapiens are biologically equal in that all races are capable of interbreeding and similar in intelligence, "in-," and "out-," groups are circumscribed by racial signs and symbols, i.e., physiological and cultural differences attributable to social status.

As the political paradigm of Power has expanded the secular domain of human motive, thereby forcing the *sacred* into the realm of the supernatural paradigm, organized religion has lost much of its impetus for forming in- and out-groups, therein. In addition, the Powerful socializing influence of state-sponsored "political correctness" has deflated *public* intergroup divisiveness. Even so, organized religion remains a dominant source for ideological differences between groups and individuals, e.g., *excommunication*, i.e., noncommunication, noncommunion, noncommunity, noncommonality, non*consubstantiality*, was, and still is, a penalty for religious ideological dissent.

A sports fan is a status wherein each and every particular "sport" constitutes a particular status unto itself. Within some cultural contexts, a "Good" citizen and a devout sports fan may be conflated, as one's social status is determined and maintained via a "fanatical" knowledge, participation, and devotion to a particular sport.

Indeed, significant lines of division occur between *teams* within a sport and between differing *terms* within sport, e.g., "sport" *as* "hunting" can alternately be interpreted as: "needless destruction and affliction of violence upon nature in the name of entertainment."

Similarly, such a *seemingly* insignificant status as a pet owner can divide communities across lines of *type* of pet, *purpose*, and *context*.

Exotic wild animals roaming semi-freely about an estate are typically signs of higher social status, while musty rodents in small cages in a trailer park denote a somewhat lesser status.

If we might digress momentarily, we may question any construction such as, "pet," e.g., what is the meaning of "pet," and if it is in some manner relatable to that action of petting as a form of aesthetic intimacy with an animal, is the term equally attributable to a scorpion or porcupine fish? Is the construction "pet" merely an expression of a desire to anthropomorphize animals as surrogate human-like confidants which do not judge, are loyal, and subservient?

If an individual is a pet owner who claims to be a "lover of animals," what form of "love" is expressed through systematically breeding animals in captivity such that they become genetically inferior and prone to latent diseases and maladies and deprived of their natural environments? Or is "pet love" actually more akin to purification through the nonjudgmental approval of animals?

Within the social construction, "food," what is food and what is not? Within which contexts does it become food? Which foods represent a status of health versus one of economy or convenience? How is food to be eaten, in which contexts, or for what purposes?

What is "art" as a function of status? Almost any possession or commodity can be divided across utilitarian and aesthetic qualities. Perhaps nothing is more subjective than art, although it is ostensibly highly implicated in social status.

Anything attributable to human value can be implicated somehow within either an in-group or out-group belief or activity in relation to social status due to the subjective and contradictory nature of language.

Language creates community out of biological-familial relationships as a result of our need for consubstantiation with others (Axioms 17, 18, 19, and 20). Through consubstantiation, i.e., community and language, we are capable of pursuing innumerable interests and activities (acts).

If the motive of consubstantiality were purely egalitarian and based in the "Good" of equality, there would not exist "in" and "out" groups within communities or society. All would be shared equally without regard to status, and individuals would not be divided by oppositional meanings and interpretations.

The need for consubstantiality exists *because* subjective (non-substantial) language allows for divisions of phenomena (Axiom 3) into subjective categories of "Good," and evil. Ironically, it is only through communication that we establish community. If we continuously throw mud against the wall, some will eventually stick. Within this "mud" we find (some) love and belonging, i.e., consubstantiation, as a manifest motive of Power *over* subjectivity and ourselves.

Ego (Self-Esteem)

According to Burke, our ultimate motive is to rid ourselves of language-induced guilt in order to achieve redemption and rise in the social hierarchy. In this sense, ego, i.e., *self*-esteem, is a primary motive behind all motives, within the political paradigm.

"Good" and "evil" are merely subjective positive and negative terms we assign to objects and concepts of *value*. That which the reader may deem as "Good" this writer may (or may not) also deem as "Good" (valuable), e.g., water. However, no matter what object or concept, we can never assign precisely the same "Good" or evil value due to differential contexts, standpoints, and interpretations.

An individual living in an extremely arid environment may come to nearly worship water as a "God term," whereas an individual residing in a geographic location which receives six feet of precipitation per year would perhaps not be *as* zealous in terms of the "Goodliness" of water.

However, the God term of all God terms, *God,* in English, has a much higher valence than all lesser constructions. Therefore, the concept of "Good," creates guilt within individuals who, through communication and social interaction, become manifestly aware of their polluted statuses in relation to the highest conceivable "Good," i.e., *God."*

The individual is essentially driven by the animalistic drives of the sexual paradigm (Axiom 23) which in the political paradigm becomes deemed the "will" which is driven by the motives of need and desire. As the individual develops, social awareness increases with respect to the needs of the self in relation to the needs of others and the intimate relationships therein.

It becomes evident to the individual that just as some value or judgment of "Good" or "evil" is assigned to objects and concepts, so too does the individual assign values of "Good" and "evil" to others, just as others to the individual.

Likewise, it becomes evident that reward is related to "Good" evaluations of the individual as punishment is related to "evil" (Axiom 7). Eventually it is realized that all human value is reducible to social value, and that the individual's ratio of "Good," in relation to the greater social economy, is intimately implicated in reward and punishment within the political and supernatural paradigms.

The ego desires the highest of "Good" evaluations by others since these translate into the highest rewards to the individual. That is not to suggest that the desires of the individual are separate from society such that the individual is totally apathetic to the needs and desires of all others. Just as young lovers share in and promote the positive emotions of love within each other (Axioms 9, 17, 14, 18, and 20), the ego shares and builds upon the positive emotions of others as it recognizes the "Good" of self in others.

However, the will of the individual preexists the ego which develops in *response* to the action of the will. It is from initial self-interest that the ego comes to be. The Good of the society is also driven by the collective will of the people, therefore society does not reach out and esteem the individual in the absence of acts of "Goodness" on behalf of the individual.

The "Goodness" of a given society, just as the "Goodness" of the individual, is relative, e.g., the ego of the individual may suffer if the Goodness of a given society does not match that of the individual in the same manner that a society is not enhanced by an individual of questionable "Goodness."

Ever since the gauntlet of "Goodness" was thrown down by the knight of symbolic language, there is no escaping the Burke-ian *guilt-redemption cycle*. All wish to rise in the social hierarchy and become "purified" as the most deserving of society. The individual is driven toward redemption through giving "voice" either through communication or through action in status (Axioms 21, 16, 4, and 14).

As society evolves, the quest for purification intensifies as new meanings and symbols replace older ones, which themselves become contested by the ego in the never-ending drama of life (Axiom 22).

By definition, the ego is vested in empowerment of the self. The "self" as becoming, as equal with others, is in tension with the *esteemed* self, i.e., the self that is lacking and therefore in need of esteem. The ego may give rise to latent "Good" in the form of utilitarianism but is manifestly rotten with perfection and endlessly seeks purification, ie., Power *over* subjectivity."

Potentiality (Self-Actualization)

Unlike *acquisition, control, and synthesis* (SAT model, Appendix I), which represent acts, *potentiality* represents a *status* of Power (Appendix V) as a function of these processes in the form of potential Power or capacity and is analogous to the supernatural paradigm of Power.

When potentiality intercepts purpose, a new level of acquisition is achieved (either natural or symbolic Truth) within subjectivity (Appendix V). The cycle continues in response to *subjectivity*. Within the field of subjectivity Power represents the capacity to act *in spite of resistance* in acquiring still greater Power, i.e., potentiality.

As we become empowered over the lower subjectivities, i.e., physiological, material, social, personal, etc., our motives evolve toward greater potentialities, i.e., of freedom, independence, creativity, ultimate Good, and by default, *unsubjectivity*.

Symbolic language allows us to imagine and conceive of the highest of potentialities, i.e., God, immortality, eternal bliss, the absence of opposition, and unsubjectivity. Therefore, we have conceived of Gods and ultimate expressions of Good for thousands of years.

Supernatural institutions such as mysticism and religion have arisen in response to our ability to conceive of higher potentialities of being and serve as symbolic liaisons between our highest aspirations and our contemporary subjectivities.

The symbolic world of the political paradigm is composed of a hierarchy of individuals competing over who gets what. This fundamental "what" is reducible to symbolic Power, i.e., potentiality. Ostensibly, all individuals would prefer to obtain the highest possible potentiality for the least amount of risk or effort. However, those lower in the political paradigm with less potential Power are more "*vested*" in the grindstones set before them as their source of potentiality, even though they may be equally motivated. Their status within the hierarchy shifts their locus of motives towards the *acts* implicated in pursuit of potentiality (working class values), i.e., acquisition, control, and synthesis.

Those higher in the hierarchy who have inherited or achieved greater potentiality can afford to enlist *others* to perform more of the laborious and complex tasks while realizing more potential Power themselves. These are they who are free to increasingly focus their attention exclusively upon potentiality.

Above these are those who are motivated solely by empowerment as the means to all other motives. These are they who are at the highest acquiring end of Power who merely discharge Power in the interest of *their* highest Truth, i.e., their *will to Power over all subjectivity.*

Traditionally, shaman and religious leaders presided over communal potentiality where the supernatural paradigm represented the greatest human mystery and therefore offered the greatest paradigm of hope and respect. Therefore, the supernatural paradigm is an ancient paradigm of Power which has controlled the workings of the masses for millennia.

With the increase of commerce and trade, secular rulers have usurped the divine right of kings as a function of the motive of potentiality. Even so, Powerful religious factions have held on to their respective stakes within the over-arching and Powerful, paradigm of the supernatural. So Powerful is this paradigm that even during the most deplorable of times in medieval history, while immaculate edifices were being constructed and clergy adorned themselves in finery, parishioners who lived lives of abject poverty and hardship *faithfully* exhausted their lives' energies in diligent service, even as the faithful masses of today - where religion remians "the opiate of the people"—Marx.

Mystification and ritual are Powerful tools of the supernatural paradigm. The meaning behind subjective sacred symbols is concealed and ambiguous to the *masses,* where ritual and tradition work instead to create emotional cohesion in lieu of logic or reason, e.g., sacred European texts were often written in obscure Latin requiring translation for the lay masses.

Just as the divine right of kings was usurped in the past, the instruments of mystification and ritual have been usurped by contemporary secular rulers, i.e., mystification through code (*also* rooted in Latin) and social constructions of meaning, i.e., what *lawfully* constitutes a "person," "citizen," "social status," "political reality," e.g., "A world wholly demystified is a world wholly depoliticized"(Clifford Geertz).

The supernatural paradigm is founded upon, and capitalized through the precept of "belief" (Axiom 11). A belief in a "moral reality," *existing independent of language and human consciousness,* is *essential* to the supernatural paradigm. In the absence of *belief* in an objective, external "reality" which is ruled over by anthropomorphic deities of "Good," and "evil" i.e., Gods and demons, there is no ultimate authority outside of subjective language upon which to base power.

According to our Axiom 14, *all meaning* is socially constructed. As the paradigm of potentiality, the supernatural paradigm is the ultimate authority in the construction of meaning. Our "reality" therefore is implicated within the cultural and linguistic constructions of the overarching supernatural, e.g., the meaning of "mortality," "sacrifice," "sin," "authority," etc.

If all reality is merely a social construction, then the supernatural paradigm serves as the authoritative master narrative which legitimizes political narratives of "reality" in the political paradigm. Meaning is established through narratives and ritual practices such as marital rights designed to bestow authority, i.e., legitimacy and social status upon individuals while *reifying* the authority of those empowered.

The basic *structure* of Western society is dictated by supernatural narratives of meaning, e.g., we are confused in the concept of time (Axiom 29) by a nonsensical, incongruent Gregorian calendar organized around holidays, i.e., "holy" days, and structure our lives according to an arbitrary (though highly symbolic) seven-day "workweek."

One may discover that many of the narratives, signs, and symbols of contemporary supernatural institutions were borrowed from earlier ones, e.g., in Christianity, there are *twelve disciples* which are analogous to the *twelve houses* of the zodiac (Egyptian astrotheology) which "helped" the Sun (son) on its (his) yearly cycle throughout the heavens. The Sun (son) appears to "die" upon the "cross" of the zodiac for three days during the winter solstice (the *apparent* motion of the Sun on the cross of the Zodiac to ancient peoples), then appears to "arise" again restoring life to crops and the people.

Narratives of many contemporary supernatural institutions are oriented in times when human interface with deities and miracles were alleged to have occurred real time amongst living flesh and blood historical characters within specific geographic locations. Ostensibly, all such supernatural interfaces have ceased such that all we are left with are narratives and symbols. Thus our supernatural paradigm of Power is based upon an epistemology of the *symbolic,* and a system of knowing based in *belief.*

How we know *what* to believe is utterly dependent upon the authority of those who *are empowered* within the paradigm of Power. Likewise, how we come to know *who* to believe is also dependent upon those who are most empowered within our supernatural paradigm.

If the motive of the supernatural paradigm were based in moral "Good" and equality of all, we should not expect to see *any* evidence of request or desire for tribute, and neither should we expect to see any differentiation in social status or hierarchy (within these institutions). Neither should we witness fanciful edifices nor material holdings, nor the use and acceptance of "legal" fiat monies as a medium of tribute (tithes) in the name of a God.

Alternatively we *should* expect to see donated time and knowledge and resources to be distributed equally *as possible* independent of secular, profane, and materialistic resources, i.e., debt, fiat money *as* debt, etc. We should not expect "True," morally legitimized institutions to accept any benefits and/or privileges from the bankrupt state (as debtor to the money changers). We *should* expect "True" and moral institutions to be *sovereign, honest,* and *self-reliant.*

Over thousands of years of human history, men and women have been aware of the Power of potentiality due to symbolic language, and therefore have sought its highest offices where one lives by the sweat of the brows of others. If there exists a moral "Good" based in the authority of an all-Powerful being, perhaps we would find such a non-hierarchical institution based solely upon Goodness and equality. However, this writer is aware of no such institution.

Alternatively, if we seek the presence of a (nearly) all-Powerful God, it can be found in *money.* Almost unilaterally it is worshiped by individuals and institutions as the ultimate symbol of potentiality. If the Good (God) is reduced to the *Word,* and the *Word* is *God,* the most Powerful and omnipresent word is *money.* If the supernatural paradigm is reducible to symbols, the most omnipotent and fundamental symbol *is* money.

In the evolution of Power from *substantive* to *formal,* the castle is gone and the king has vanished, having been replaced by mere form. Any clear and present danger the king or his castle may have once represented has been replaced with innocuous symbols, rituals, and beliefs.

Whereas the political paradigm has evolved from a more or less collectivist society based in the exchange of substance, i.e., goods and services, we now are suspended within an individualistic postmodern society of symbols where media *is* community and we are reduced to consumers and producers of mediated culture where the value (substance) of the individual is replaced by the value of symbols (form) and the ultimate motive of potentiality is money.

If graffiti on public and private edifices is an effort on the part of the dispossessed to *symbolically* reclaim "turf" from the dominant Powers that be, we should not be surprised to see a rise in the tattoo as a symbolic effort (by the symbol using and abusing animal) to quell the anomie of the individual in reclaiming the last remaining form of substance (the human body), however ironically, *through signs and symbols*; the final arbiters of potentiality in pursuit of our unsubjectivity.

SECTION III

Conclusion

Supernatural Power

If anything matters, which we have argued affirmatively (although we acknowledge a compelling argument in favor of determinism wherein we have *no* choice either way), and *if* giving voice is in any way related to arriving at consensus in relation to matters of exigency between individuals, and *if* giving voice is the only logical way of obtaining knowledge in the form of *acquiring* voice, and *if* the act of giving voice promotes equality of voice, i.e., Power *with*, and *if* giving voice is or should be the most fundamental human right, and *if* in fact it is a right, and *if* an idea is met with expressed or tacit agreement and said agreement constitutes a legitimate contract, then this essay constitutes the endeavor of *this* writer to give voice to his views in relation to his personal standpoint for the purpose of acquiring and sharing voice in pursuit of the highest Good in relation to human purpose.

It is acknowledged that the theories, axioms, and evolutionary perspective chosen biases all other assumptions as well as our final conclusion. Additionally, section II (analysis) represents more of an index of "talking points" than a comprehensive, "scholarly" discourse as a template for more comprehensive, less biased discourses. Even though we have attempted to construct a logical hierarchy of motives in order to organize related ideas using Maslow's hierarchy of needs as a model, motives could be grouped under *any* related nomenclature *and* any motive could be more logically connected with any other motive depending on context.

It is equally recognized that any motives or submotives circumscribed herein are relative to the particular standpoint of this writer since a comprehensive listing and analysis of submotives could not be explored in an individual's lifetime, therefore it is necessary to default to the task of giving voice according to *standpoint theory*.

In this section, we consider the Pyramid of Power from the top down as more analogous to social structure than a hierarchy of motives as it relates to human purpose.

As has already been elucidated in our *subjective annihilation theory*, as per the *big bang theory*, all arrows of human motivation point toward an undefined point (pointing forward rather than backward) which we call subjective annihilation (annihilation of subjectivity). Over millennia of symbolic evolution, the *ultimate* goal of humans has been canonized in narratives of Goodness and *Power*, i.e., the ultimate attainment of all things Good inclusive of love, and immunity to pain and death. If there *are* higher desires then these, they remain obscured to this writer, excepting of course, annihilation of subjectivity.

For most humans, the ostensible highest manifestation *of* Good is some form of "God" (which is represented as the pinnacle of our Pyramid of Power). Often, this force or Power is described as *all-Powerful*. It is *this* ultimate conception of Good which breaks down and implodes upon itself. It is a construction of paradoxes, i.e., if God is all-Powerful *and* Good, how could she/he/it allow evil to exist, and *why* would she/he/it?

God *could* allow evil to exist because she/he/it is all-Powerful. God may do whatever she/he/it wills. If God may do whatever she/he/it wills, under what moral *obligation*, and to whom, *must* God be "Good?" If God is all-Powerful, could she/he/it not just as easily be evil, and what possible difference would it make, and to whom? Who stands in judgement of an all-Powerful God?

An all-Powerful being would be something we could not know or describe through *symbolic language*. All-Powerful is a description of something *oppositional* to other things and conditions, i.e., the *absence of Power.* We use a term to construct and describe our highest Good which *annihilates* reason.

At this juncture, it seems redundant to attempt to analyze that which is unanalyzable through language, however, to continue in our digression, what need or lack would cause an all-Powerful God to create the universe? We digress toward absurdity by trying to suppose that God was perhaps lonely or bored. However, any motive to cause something *other* to be negates an all-Powerful God, if only logically.

A less than all-Powerful "God" is somewhat more reasonable. Such a God makes sense in relation to evolution if we consider God as having evolved out of nature or some preexisting condition. The difficulties we encounter here are the problems of subjectivity, i.e, "God" is subject to *other things and conditions,* and the origin of "God," which ironically brings us back to evolution as the mechanism of creation.

What we encounter is a *lack of definition,* and by extension, an unknown or unknowable being. Unless we know God's relation to Power and therefore Power *over* "Good" and "evil," we exist in a "diluted" universe of relative "Goodness." Whatever constitutes this marginal "Goodness" could run the gamut from a merely symbolic God evoked by symbolic construction, to a semi all-Powerful God.

However, now we are discussing linguistic *descriptions* and *definitions* of God, and it is here that we arrive at the crux of the God "idiom," i.e., all religions have particular definitions and narratives regarding who and what their "God" is and does. If there were only one True God who is permanent, perpetual, and eternal, then all descriptions would coincide exquisitely.

Believers who ascribe to a less than all-Powerful God must ostensibly construct narratives and conjectures to fill in the gaps of reason in order to exonerate their Gods. It is an inconvenient paradox to worship a God of diminished, limited, or unknowable "Good." One apology might form along such lines as: "Although God is not *all-Powerful,* he *is* our creator and therefore we should worship him as such."

Perhaps we can accept such oversimplifications, however, *this* begs the question: *How is it that we come to know such things?* i.e., this less then all-Powerful God as our creator if she/he/it is not the *absolute* arbiter of Truth, particularly if such knowledge arrives to us *secondhand* by the arm and tongue of the flesh through symbolic language?

If God represents the highest Good relative to humans, what *fundamental* Truth exists, and where—outside of subjective language, which guides us to ask the *correct* questions at the *optimal* time, in the *appropriate* context, of the *correct* agents, in order to arrive at the "correct" Truth?

Another simplification might be that the Spirit moves within and guides us. If this is so, we might rejoice even though we still do not understand the fundamental basis or motive for the Spirit's involvement and why such involvement, or not, *seems* random and prejudicial amongst individuals who were ostensibly created "equal" *by* God.

Some knowledge *is* accessible however, i.e., the knowledge which the *individual* or *agent* is transmitting through *symbolic language* explaining the "how-to's" of God. However, this seems analogous to how we gain secular knowledge, e.g., a teacher or instructor instills knowledge regarding the "how-to's" of speaking, reading, writing, etc., through *symbolic communication*. The spirit *may* here, too, be working from within, however this knowledge is ostensibly transferred (unapologetically) through symbolic language alone.

We also have *cultural knowledge* which, is transferred through symbolic language, including any traditions and values unique to a particular culture, e.g., most cultures have instilled the tradition and value of wearing clothes, therefore, how do we know to wear clothes? The symbolically instilled *cultural spirit moves within us* guiding us to get dressed before going into public domain.

The "Spirit," may *still* be the source of *all action* whether wearing clothes or in worshipping a God. However, lke marionettes we still do not know the nature of "God" i.e., all-Powerful, sort-of-Powerful, angry, benevolent, literal, symbolic, etc., in order to acknowledge and worship the *Truthful* God.

Alternatively, if all men are created equal and the Spirit moves equally through all men, we needn't worship, understand, fight, nor argue in the name of a God, since God is that she/he/it is, and therefore moves unabridged through all men as she/he/it wilt.

Each individual culture necessarily believes that its version of God or Gods is the more true and correct, therefore belief in God or Gods is necessarily always from *within a cultural perspective*, and therefore worshipping a God or Gods from within a cultural tradition or perspective is equivalent to disparaging (polluting) the highest Good of differing cultures. Who or what God is to any given culture consists in its narratives and stories (symbolic language) linking said culture to its specific version of the ultimate Good.

Ultimately then, God consists within *descriptions* of the highest Power of Good with respect to ethnological origin through symbolic language, i.e., God is *the Word*.

God *may* in fact be all-Powerful, semi-Powerful, more or less good or evil, angry, good-humored, or even a flying spaghetti monster which works in mysterious ways through miracles and supernatural powers. However, *prior* to all of these constructions, God is evoked *as* a word, is come to be known *through* words, and is advocated by the word.

If communication *is* the process of differentiating "Good" from "evil" through the assignment of value to things and conditions by circumscribing phenomena as meaningful, i.e., generally Good or bad, *and* symbolic language allows us to artificially reconstruct "reality," then it is neither confusing nor perplexing if we should create Gods in our own image as symbolic of ultimate expressions of "Good" and "evil." Such constructions seem not only logical and reasonable, but given the nature of symbolic language—*inevitable*.

If God *is* the Word and therefore a function of symbolic language and this writer were asked, "Do *you* believe in God?" He would answer with an unequivocal, "*Yes!*" However, language is subjective in nature and therefore has no *intrinsic* meaning, as such words are culturally disseminated like Trojan horses imbued with culturally biased meanings which strategically ambush their receivers.

A commonsense orientation to experience and meaning preserves a sort of culturally simplistic and generalized relationship with knowledge, e.g., if someone were to ask *this* writer, "Do *you* believe in

UFOs?" He would answer unequivocally, "*Yes!*" However, the problem with UFOs is the problem with God. It seems possible, if not probable, that due to the construction of such a question, the interrogator has culturally imbued "UFOs" with "little green men" and extraterrestrial spacecraft and conspiracy theories, et al.

This writer *unequivocally* believes in unidentified flying objects *and* frequently encounters them. Often they turn out to be common ordinary aircraft, yet even after landing, they often remain unidentified, i.e., make, model, engine type, fuel type, proper nomenclature of identification, etc., therefore, perhaps, they become USOs.

This writer does not however, subscribe to such constructions as "little green men," "Bigfoots," "Loch Ness monsters," "conspiracy theories," etc. The hollow signifier "God" is likewise imbued with cultural meaning and disseminated colloquially. For that matter, all terms and gestures are hollow signifiers dependent upon cultural understanding and context e.g., when we say, "Good morning," is it *really* a "*Good*" morning above all others things which might possibly be evoked, or is it, "I come in peace and wish no trouble with you, and if you give me trouble, it is you, not I, who provoked it." Is the military salute purely a formal expression of respect, or is it a leftover cultural reflex of identity as per earlier times when a knight would raise his visor to identify himself?

Therefore, this writer's culturally imbued description of *his* God is as follows: in the beginning was the Word, and the Word divided the world betwixt that which was Good and that which was evil (since that which is Good is to be acquired while that which is evil is to be avoided), and after many dispensations, those things which were deemed of the highest Good were coveted and given unto the name, *Goodness*, i.e., food, resources, health, wealth, family, etc. Those things which were consistently bad came to symbolize evil (vileness), i.e., a lack of food and resources, and those things which might challenge or threaten, the Good, i.e., drought, dwindling resources, sickness, death, liars, cheaters, thieves, deceivers, enemies, etc.

Those who controlled the symbols and wrote the narratives of a society, i.e., priests and scribes, deified the "Good" and "evil" of their particular societies as above and beyond the realm of men as the highest expression of their cultural values.

Thus these *men* created "Gods" in their own image as the ultimate authorities and expressions of Power, thereby becoming the ultimate arbiters of Power through the Gods they created.

Since Gods are born and made meaningful through *descriptions based in symbolic language*, the best description of the most Powerful God must be the Truest God. A less than all-Powerful God is more coherent than a paradoxical "all-Powerful God," however, a less than all-Powerful God is equivocal, undefined, and unknowable. If what God is and does is dependent upon the elucidations of men, through symbolic language, whomever controls the *descriptions* of God, *is* God.

However, it is not the descriptions of God themselves which create Gods out of men, but the ultimate control over society's *highest symbols* through the Gods they create. Gods throughout history have nearly always been perched on the shoulders of the rulers of a society. If the "God's" manifest motive were morality in the form of equality, fairness, and humility, one would not expect the Gods to so consistently align themselves with cultural elitism and hierarchy.

However, the Gods have more exigent functions beyond mere morality, they also function to preserve the hierarchical status quo through ultimate authority and as a scapegoat mechanism. Suddenly, any perplexing, incongruent paradoxes with respect to the Gods, mysticism, religion, and the *supernatural paradigm*, seem to melt away. If social reality is merely a construction, not inevitable, nor carved in stone, and is composed through subjective language, then to make it appear otherwise *is* Power.

To have the capability to control the construction of "reality" and preserve it is crucial to a hierarchical structure. Any inevitable paradoxes or incongruences arising therein due to subjective language and counter-interests are easily deferred into the lap of the Gods, e.g., "All men are *created* equal." Therefore, the highest *knowable* God is man (humans) as the maker of the Word and the Word *as* God.

If religious institutions were more concerned with issues of morality than hierarchical structuring, rather than soliciting tribute (through fiat monies) in the form of tithes and offering, they might instead seek other forms of value such as donation of durable goods and volunteer labor.

Rather then building fine edifices and acquiring assets and real estate holdings (tax free), they might liquidate such assets and distribute resources to the most needy and establish instead efficacious networks of volunteer service and production.

However, the scapegoat mechanism of mysticism and religion effectively shifts guilt away from men (sexist languaging saved in context as standard nomenclature within this subject matter) and into the lap of the Gods, thereby enabling narratives of reward and punishment (in relation to social status) to justify the incongruencies of "morality."

If one was generally familiar with one's cultural prescriptions of morality, and they included such concepts as charity, sympathy, and equality, and such an individual was having a outdoor barbecue and happened to notice what appeared to be an emaciated homeless individual passing by, this individual would likely either ignore the ostensibly homeless individual, or attempt to offer food or other relief due to culturally instilled guilt.

As linguistic animals, it is nearly impossible to socially interact and *not* become exposed to all social constructions of the "Good," bad, and the ugly, therefore we learn to identify (to a high degree) familiar cultural constructions such as the "homeless," or "disadvantaged," etc.

Because of our guilt-enabling language (knowledge of Good and evil), we feel implicated and uneasy when publicly confronted with overt moral confluences of incongruity (such as per our neighborhood chef) when *we* encounter others who appear less fortunate. We feel *publicly* compelled to donate while our expensive gas-guzzling automobile idles next to the ostensibly out-of-work veteran, and if we don't capitulate we must somehow divert our attention not as motorists or "travelers," but as *guilt-ridden, language-sharing, moral beings.*

We cannot escape a language-caused moral sense of guilt when we encounter such incongruencies. We must reconstruct the situation so as to either mitigate guilt or capitulate. By default, we *prefer* others to witness our capitulation as a public act of guilt-purging on our behalf. In this manner, an ostensible manifest act of public charity becomes a latent act of guilt-purging.

However, it may in fact be the case that the homeless individual above has lost her/his job and/or profession directly due to competitive and perhaps even unscrupulous acts on behalf of the organization which is the benefactor of our neighborhood chef. Such very real structural, moral, and ethical incongruencies (of technologies) would soon overwhelm and *subsume* us if there were not a scapegoat mechanism to purge us of our guilt.

By organizationally dumping such conundrums into the lap of the "Gods," we are able to navigate a world of moral contradictions as though it were perfectly ordained. The Gods enable us to build our castles upon the crushed bones of the less fortunate with immaculate entitlement.

The Power of the *supernatural paradigm* is *mystification*. It is Good for political Power to have its ultimate authority based upon a *hollow signifier*. In this manner, she/he who has control of the ultimate symbols (of Good) can imbue them with whatever meaning she/he desires. Therefore, Gods who are unknowable, or "work in mysterious ways" serve as perfect scapegoat mechanisms. All-Powerful symbols are imbued with mystification such that they arouse Powerful emotional allegiance based in the supernatural. The Power of the supernatural paradigm is that "reality" is as putty in the hands of the elite.

If this writer were asked, "Do *you* believe in God?" He would answer with an unequivocal, "*Yes!*" *If* God consists of the most *reasonable* description of the most Powerful known being, then humans *are* God, the highest manifestation of which is represented in the individual with the greatest control over symbolic meaning, i.e., [he] who controls the highest symbols of value.

Even though this essay is based upon the premise that *evolution* is the mechanism of creation, this writer chooses to capitalize the word *God* (other than for rhetorical purposes) herein since according to the standpoint of this writer, humans *are* (Gods). Therefore, as the highest known manifestations of Power, respect is due of the Gods in their various manifestations of their highest Truths until *proven otherwise*.

Additionally, this writer does not *assume* that anyone's "God" or construction thereof is false, not even a flying spaghetti monster. It is a naive and commonsense orientation which leads to impetuous reactions and assumptions, i.e., it is naive to assume that anyone can *prove* anything beyond conditions of *context* (although it is possible to contextually refine "gravities" of Truth through reasoned analysis).

It is very difficult to prove that even a flying spaghetti monster does *not* exist in some form, nor ever could. However, relative to more reasonable constructions, such a monster ostensibly has a relatively low gravity of Truth outside of a symbolic construction.

Many realities *may* in fact exist independent of language, the difficulty is *how* we come to know them *outside* of language. We may sense impressions or intuitions (certainly humans have instincts), however, they are interpreted and made meaningful through and within the context of symbolic language.

Ironically, the existence of an all-Powerful *benevolent* and *just* being may be of the highest aspiration for any self-described *"outsider-artist-philosopher"* types who dwell just beyond the "Roche limit" of impetuous social interactions where an ostensible collectivist commonsense filter and scapegoat mechanism works to enable individuals to boldly "surf" contradiction in order to maximize personal reward. However, for *this* self-described "outsider," even a paradoxical "all-Powerful" God is of limited consolation if she/he/it, too, is ostensibly *subject to other things and conditions*.

Unsubjectivity

As the highest manifestation of the Truth of Goodness and Power over subjectivity, our supernatural paradigm represents the paradigm of *the meaning of meaning* (meta-symbolic) where the symbolic eye of gnosis resides at its peak representing the greatest knowledge.

Our quest for the highest Truth of Good and Power is dynamic and perpetual and drives the entire paradigm of Power, thus the highest point of confluence between the Good and the Powerful (could fluctuate anywhere between points (d) and (e) on our *Truth, Power, and Good* model appendix V) continuously ascends toward unsubjectivity.

Our model (Appendix V) represents a static balance of motives and forces in relation to Truth, however, we would argue that the motive of Good in nature (food, sex, homeostasis, etc.) is evolving from point (c) toward point (b) as a singular motive of Power (the will to Power over subjectivity) as technology subsumes nature. Thus Truth valence would shift accordingly from point (a) toward point (d) thus producing a *right,* as opposed to the *equilateral triangle* as depicted in Appendix V. Once all subjectivities of nature are overcome by empowerment and we are left with only a trajectory from point (b) to point (d), we are approaching *Subjective Annihilation*.

Perhaps it is impossible for humans, and even less than all-Powerful Gods to completely escape subjectivity, however, even if this were discoverable as categorical fact, it does not appear in any way to annihilate our collective evolutionary will towards unsubjectivity.

Our highest symbolic representation of unsubjectivity is encapsulated within narratives of an all-Powerful God. Such cultural narratives of archaic descent underscore a *fundamental human psychology* rooted in an ultimate desire for *unsubjectivity.*

We have previously examined the difficulties with a paradoxical all-Powerful God in relation to subjectivity and how belief in such constructions creates subjectivities thereto through mystification of the hollow signifier, i.e., God, which may be manipulated meaningfully in the interests of its gatekeepers.

A creationist view of "unsubjectivity" creates a false consciousness based upon self-annihilating and unknowable Gods which in turn are used to subject individuals to things and conditions external to their individual wills, e.g., as per *the Wonderful Wizard of Oz.*

From a commonsense perspective, an individual may assert that he or she does not really wish to be "unsubject" *to everything*, i.e., that they would like to be subject to love and eternal bliss, however, love exists in opposition to hate, and bliss to misery, whereas *unsubjectivity* must necessarily be a state of *no opposition*, the only *reasonable* state of an all-Powerful God. A less than all-Powerful God or a human God is subject to other things and conditions leaving our problem of subjectivity open-ended, waiting to be annihilated by our voracious will to Power over subjectivity.

A creationist view also fosters a *noncritical,* communal orientation to meaning and purpose, i.e., an all-Powerful God is illogical, while a less than all-Powerful God is counterintuitive and dependent upon *descriptions* (just as human Gods) in order to be meaningful yet can only be known *through* the hand and tongue of the flesh. If our highest human purpose is to live in eternal bliss with God, such is a purpose of *paradox.* Since an "all-Powerful" God would not exist in a state of opposition to other things and conditions, i.e., evil, therefore, to live in "Goodness" with "God" necessitates a state of "evilness" as an oppositional counterpart within subjectivity. in the absence of "evil," "Goodness" becomes meaningless.

A creationist view therefore implicates a *necessitous* and *eternal* relationship with "evil." We are created "equal," but through some mystical Power some of us become "corrupted" such that while the saints are dwelling in eternal bliss in heaven, a necessitous parallel existence of "sinners," i.e., children, aunts, uncles, cousins, brothers, lovers, must *simultaneously* burn in hell for *eternity*.

Alternatively, if humans are God and symbolic language *is* the Word, the innumerable ways in which *we* pollute and purify one another according to differential interpretations of "Good" versus "evil" becomes exceedingly evident (the various *mystical* and *religious* narratives mirror such antagonisms exquisitely). In this light, it does not seem surprising that emphasis is centered upon *belief* rather than moral *"Goodness."*

Scores of narratives, apologies, explanations, nuances, and idiosyncrasies spawned by a creationist perspective could (and does) fill volumes of literature generating endless perplexities and debate over many centuries and numerous competing factions.

Subjective Annihilation Theory merely suggests that the individual does not wish to be subject to other things and conditions outside of her/his will, thus she/he seeks to reduce and eliminate them. There is *no known boundary nor limit* of the will in relation to subjectivity, thus the end result by default can only be—*annihilation of subjectivity*.

In comparison to an anthropomorphic all-Powerful-being, Subjective Annihilation Theory may not seem appeasing since it does not *assuage the human ego*, additionally, it is unknown and perhaps unknowable whether annihilation of subjectivity is even possible. However, it does provide an efficient and simple methodology for arriving at gravities of Truth in relation to individuals, societies, and human motivation.

Everything we do is in response to subjectivity. If reality is not carved in stone and dependent upon adherence to mystical ideals as a creationist view would advocate, and we are not helpless marionettes living in a demon-haunted world, then understanding subjectivity is essential to reasoned and purposeful action.

Contemporary subjectivity is analogous to debt (*and often entails debt*). We find ourselves in need of things to live and be contented, and in as far as we have insufficient resources, we seek Power in acquiring external resources through which to satiate our needs and desires. This in turn necessitates expenditure of time and energy *apart* from our natural will to "Good."

Many people are enslaved by debt for which they have forgotten its initial (Good) purpose, particularly as they continuously rollover and consolidate it. Likewise it is within subjectivity, actions and agreements which were initially precipitated by *our will* to Good become actions and agreements *in compromise* with the will of others.

Whether debt or subjectivity in general, all human interaction is ultimately a battle of the wills, e.g., the banker wishes to divert the individual's will to Good in favor of his *interest*, just as individuals seek to protect their own. Those with both a strong will and *voice* are formidable opponents, i.e., organizations, corporations, social institutions, the wealthy, etc. The will of the Powerful is inordinate and likewise wishes to subjugate the will of the less Powerful toward their own best *interests*. Thus hollow signifiers, i.e., God, and false consciousness, as in, "All men are *created* equal," are Powerful tools for usurping the will of the individual in favor of the *will of the Powerful.*

However, unlike the necessitous and incestuous paradoxical relationship between "Good" and "evil" within creation narratives, subjectivity is a *natural* component of *Subjective Annihilation Theory*. Every individual alive today has overcome extreme odds over millions of years of evolution. We were designed and engineered *by* the subjectivity of the environments and conditions of our evolutionary ancestors.

Contentment and pleasure is nature's reward for *overcoming subjectivity*. Goodness *is* victory over subjectivity. Wherever there is jubilance, exaltation, or celebration, there is the experience, or *perception of,* victory over some subjectivity. A creationist viewpoint relocates such jubilance's under the banner of supernatural Goodness, thereby giving credence to the will of God in lieu of the will to Good of individuals.

In theory, given the opportunity, we ought to manifestly (as opposed to latently) choose to become unsubject, thereby instantly freeing ourselves from all possible pain and suffering while achieving the highest state of oneness. However, we are symbol-using and abusing animals who know of nothing outside of symbolic language. We are born into, and die within, a symbolic universe of meanings constituted of "Good" and "evil." We know nothing of an existence unsubject to *anything* since it is an existence beyond symbols and language, and therefore, beyond meaning.

To die is ostensibly the nearest experience of unsubjectivity we can imagine (even if we believe energy and matter cannot be destroyed). Therefore, even if unsubjectivity is our unspoken *destiny*, at this stage in our evolution it cannot be fully appreciated, except as a theoretical trajectory with which we may dissect contemporary human motives in our unconscious pursuit thereof.

Political Power

Our political paradigm (Appendix III) represents a hierarchical as well as chronological progression of Power from bottom to top. Hierarchically, the lowest point within the paradigm represents those with the least voice and therefore influence and the highest point representing those who control the highest symbols within the paradigm. Chronologically, the lowest point of our paradigm corresponds to our earliest symbolic communication with the highest representing our most contemporary.

Ostensibly, the supernatural and political paradigms arose concurrently during the age of mysticism out of the chaos of the sexual paradigm. As technological innovations would have been relatively minimal, the highest Truth (a) in Power and Good would have been much nearer to the baseline (Appendix V), creating a relatively horizontal incline toward Truth (a).

Technology provides Power necessary for escaping subjectivity. The technology of organizing through symbolic representation is of the highest forms of Power as it provides for, and regulates, the most efficacious means of production and distribution of resources.

Innovation and quantum leaps of discovery are subsumed under the rubric of politics, as technological advantage creates tension between who gets what within the "Good" of society.

Symbolic language and the Power of organizing gives rise to an increase in innovation, however, technology, i.e., knowledge of technique, is not *freely* disseminated to the masses, therefore, a disparity of knowledge between the franchised and disenfranchised begins to grow as technology evolves.

After some time, the lay masses become so oblivious to the technological machinery of governance that they become *subsumed* within its matrix. The interests of the the ruling class becomes self-fulfilling by default in the absence of a critically informed populace.

Technological improvements in public works further engenders an apathetic public which becomes reliant upon the machinery of governance and its technological efficacy. Social stratification grows ever greater between the lay masses, the innovators, and ruling classes, as all levels of public/corporate organization become complicit within its hegemonic machinations.

Liaisons and backroom agreements form between public and private interests while the increasingly apathetic masses are entertained by bread and circus. Public interests become private interests, and de jure governments become de facto governments. The people become as chattel unto the state, as the state becomes their master.

Knowledge is Power, however, knowledge requires conscientiousness, persistence, diligence, and continuously giving and acquiring of *critical voice*. Becoming is doing (action), not merely speaking, i.e., we *are* what we do, not merely what we say. *If* all men *are* created equal, then all men should share equally in the Good of Power *with* in pursuit of unsubjectivity. However, as one political pundit once put it, "We gave you a republic... *if* you can keep it."

Communication

If reality is a social construction based upon symbolic language, then both the political and supernatural paradigms of Power are merely a subjective fabrication *symbolically* constructed of motives. If human motives are manifestly based in egalitarian Good, we should not expect to see *any* hierarchical structure as all would be shared equally. However, the term "Good" itself is a morally infused and subjective term as is, "moral."

Equality is not to be found within the pre-symbolic sexual paradigm as it is the paradigm of the "fittest." If humans evolved, rather than having been created, there is no objective, "equal" playing field upon which to establish a moral basis of merit. Therefore, we are born into a disparity of genetic and environmental circumstances just as our ancestors were. In a perfectly egalitarian society, an *equal distribution* of resources throughout the community is required in order to maintain equality.

Social hierarchy is a fact of nature which we have inherited *biologically*. Communication functions to manifestly construct hierarchies in order to *ensure* moral "Goodness" as an ordered society is more efficacious and desirable. Thus, social hierarchy is both a natural and inevitable condition of society. A society's highest *Truth* represents a balance between motives of *Power* and *Good* where hierarchy provides the motive of Power, and individual will, the motive of the Good (Appendix:V).

As long as a *reasonable* balance is maintained between hierarchy and will (a), there remains a symbiotic relationship between Power and Good, i.e., the will to individual Good without means (e) is futile thus undermining the "benefit" side of the equation. Too much Power (d) over taxes the will to Good of the individual as the matrix implodes upon itself.

The terms: communication, community, communion, etc., essentially mean to share or to share in common. The only reasonable way to ensure the highest manifest Truth of a community is *through communication*, i.e., through giving (*and* receiving) *critical* voice.

If an individual participates in *any* community, virtual or otherwise, and the highest Truth of a community consists of a reasoned balance between the will to Power and the will to Good, then it becomes a *duty* to oneself (as no one is an island) and a *social obligation* to the community to *give critical voice* to those things which one perceives as "Good" or "evil," i.e., desirable/undesirable, true/untrue.

If an individual participates in symbolic communication, then she/he is a member of a *community*. The Internet is a community *of* communities within a complex global network. At *no* time in history has the act of giving and acquiring *critical* voice been so profoundly exigent, significant, accessible, *and* essential to the Good of all.

Nothing exists outside of symbolic language wherein *Power* is required in order to overcome subjectivity. *All* human subjectivities are implicated within the Pyramid of Power, therefore a lack of *critical* voice (communication) on behalf of the individual constitutes latent support of the status quo.

If all human action is motivated by the reduction of subjectivity, organizational narratives of the supernatural paradigm function to create a false consciousness by diverting attention and energy away from an individual's subjectivity and toward acts of "faith" and "subservience" in return for symbolic purification and the protection of the Gods.

Within the political paradigm (from which there is no escape), there are innumerable written and spoken rules which require adherence by individuals which are explicit and mandatory. As per the *Wonderful Wizard of Oz,* we accept such proclamations uncritically as though they were of divine origin without regard for reason and logic.

If there is in fact a "great and Powerful wizard" or "Gods" or "spaghetti monsters" which are *overtly* or *covertly* the basis for authority and Power, these should be *vigorously* sought and *reasonably* linked to an individual's social obligation through the process of giving and acquiring *critical* voice. If any such apparitions be *reasonably* linked to authority, they should be honored and worshipped if their motives are Good. However, if such apparitions or narratives should prove *unreasonable,* or *unknowable,* any authority overtly or covertly linked to, or based upon, such apparitions should be deemed equally *unreasonable* and *unknowable* (at least until such a time as they become so).

Just as *symbolic language* is the modus operandi *through* which authority is established through rules and codes, symbolic language should equally be the litmus test *through* which we discover *supernatural justification* (or not) of authority. Authority based in *reason* is much less subject to *manipulation* than authority based in *mystification.*

If we literally *live* and *die* by the word (symbolic language), since there is no "natural" way of being in the world, we should equally be critical *of* the word *through* the word, i.e., *critical* voice, particularly *if* it is possible for individuals and entities to [re]construct Power and authority so as to *overtly* or *covertly* shift their own subjectivities onto the backs of others.

However, whether or not humans are of divine origin, there is no escaping the fact that the Pandora's box of symbolic communication has been opened such that we not only have knowledge of Good and evil, but we have the ability to *consciously choose and act upon it.*

Family

The archetype and basis of the political paradigm consists in the "family" as a function of the manifest Power of the sexual paradigm. Who gets whom at the level of the family is fundamental to the evolution of Power within the political paradigm.

It is perhaps not surprising that supernatural/creationist constructions of the "family" locate the mechanics of heterosexual coupling within narratives such as, "There is someone for everyone," or "The Lord doth provide," as though sexual union was the province of divine ordinance and a function of moral entitlement.

The supernatural paradigm has historically presided over constructions of the family in conjunction with narratives of "Good" in relation to community (society) as the primary locus of social control. The family, i.e., the sexually reproductive couple together with its offspring, is the evolutionary microcosm of the political paradigm of Power. The family is the primal human organization most fundamental to subsequent symbolic formulations of Power.

In the animal kingdom, sexual union is amongst the most *fundamental* and *natural* motives in nature giving rise to the *potential* for immortality. In the absence of successful reproduction, all else becomes meaningless. Within this context, it is not unexpected that the sexual economy would be *intensely* competitive.

If sexual coupling is a morally dependent function of entitlement, all men are *not* created morally equal unless there is always a proportional amount of sexually mature males to females *available* at any given point in time, otherwise, there must necessarily be a presumption of inequality on behalf of the creator manifest *within* said disparity, if any.

If the family is the most fundamental unit of human empowerment, then it *is* a most Powerful locus of control. Therefore, it would be in the best organizational interest for families to be of a monogamous nature, thereby ensuring a greater stability and consubstantiation. In addition, monogamous families form self-contained economic units which are more easily organized and managed.

Historical and contemporary (public) records of (predominantly male) emperors, kings, presidents, and religious leaders are *replete* with allegations and attestations of sexual audaciousness, including: lewdness, fornication, adultery, multiple concubines, rape, polygamy, etc. Juxtaposing such (*known*) sexual behaviors of dominant individuals with "family values" of the subordinate classes elucidates the Powerful and dominant motive of the *sex drive* in conjuctio with an inverted false consciousness of "morals" which is promulgated upon the masses.

Alignment with, and conformity to supernatural narratives of morality serves to reinforce the illusion that there is no sexual economy and that merely "deserving" couples are brought together divinely through prescribed associations within the moral community. In this manner, sexual competition becomes opaque and within an organizationally sponsored belief in the divinity of union.

However, within the political paradigm, the sexual economy is an intense arena of competition divided across numerous symbolically constructed dialectics of "Good" versus "evil," e.g., in nature, females defer to dominant and assertive males while males seek attributes which are conducive to reproductivity, i.e., receptiveness, healthy reproductive functioning expressed in various chemical and physical signs of normalcy. Within the symbolic political paradigm, innumerable subconstructions of compatibility occur across such diverse groupings as: social class, race, culture, religion, education, aesthetics, etc.

Innumerable constructions of pollution versus purification factor into the politics of such dialectics, e.g., the greater the disparity between social classes, the less likely a coupling, excepting of course numerous aberrations such as the disparity in aesthetics, i.e., a highly attractive female coupling with a dominant male of high position.

If we did not discriminate across race and culture, we would not be able to distinguish between races or cultures. Likewise, we would not expect to encounter any disparities between the scholarly and illiterate.

Such contradiction between categories mirrors the contradiction of symbolic language, which when coupled with aesthetics, makes for a veritable potpourri of pollutions versus purifications, e.g., depending on one's view of the human body (Grecian to Victorian, etc.) and its nature and functions, the human body is replete with sin and disgust in its natural condition and functions and must be concealed and censored or venerated and adorned depending on one's cultural orientation.

The family is the most basic and fundamental structure to the Pyramid of Power since it is the paradigm of domination and (potential) immortality upon which the pyramid is based. The family itself, by nature, is a hierarchical paradigm of specialization. Within the (symbolic) *political paradigm,* it forms a refuge and stalwart against the contradictory and exclusive symbolic hierarchy within the larger social economy. Thus the family is not only a natural construct, but a socially reconstructed paradigm of Power which by definition is *exclusive* of others.

If the manifest motive of the family were the Good of all then the distinction "family" would not exist. All would share equally in reproductive, as well as administrative functions. Emphasis would be placed upon individual Good. However, the construction, "family," which is fundamental to *natural* species, is a paradigm of Power unto itself and as such purifies and pollutes from within its battlements according to the dominant narratives of Powerful interests, such that whatever is socially imbued into the Trojan horse term, "family," serves to sustain the status quo which in turn resists any neutral or natural formations outside of its paradigm of Power.

The family is the fundamental bastion against subjectivity. At its very core is resistance to mortality expressed through successful reproduction. The most basic motives of security, food, and sex are satiated efficiently within its fundamental socioeconomic structure which forms the basis and staging area for the pursuit of all other motives. In the same manner that animals huddle together in order to weather a storm, the family provides a fortification against subjectivity, both in subjectivity to nature and subjectivity within the paradigm of Power. Thus the family constitutes a Power *over* organization within nature and society.

The Individual

As the reader may recall, this essay is contingent upon whether or not *anything* is of significance. A cursory observation of animal behavior particularly in terms of survival, food, and sex greatly suggests that to them, many things are of significance.

If evolution is the method of creation, then we, humans, must necessarily be imbued with a similar orientation to *significance*. If "reality" is predetermined which *seems* plausible, what we do in relation to consequences is perhaps morally insignificant since there is ostensibly no choice of will. In a *predetermined* universe, there is no choice in the matter, thus the only difference being the absence of a final, "moral" judgment day.

Whether by free will or fate, this writer locates "significance" within the "self" of the individual. It is the sentient body of the individual which senses and interprets signs (as per animals) as consequential, i.e., Good or bad, and it is the symbolically created mind of the self which gives meaning to significance.

The "self" therefore is not an objective and autonomous entity independent of language, but rather a social construction invoked and evoked *through* symbolic meaning. "*Sign*-ificance" originates in the prehuman animal, and significance as *self*-awareness, *social-awareness*, and ultimate *purpose*, is second-tier significance as a function of *symbolic language* and the *reciprocal* social construction of reality.

163

As the first-tier locus of significance, the individual presents the most reasonable, logical, and ethical basis for reconstructing the *Good* of humanity, i.e., empathy, equality, shared Power, etc. *All* humans begin life as *non*-symbol-using animals utterly incapable of "immoral" acts and therefore symbolically pure and innocent.

The only motives of pre-symbolic infants are located within the Good of nature (Appendix V). In essence, we are all united in the same basic motives of infancy, i.e., food, security, affection. Only after we learn to use symbols are we capable of becoming corrupted by greed as we learn to manipulate (abuse) symbols to our advantage.

In nature, the state of infancy is left to the roll of the dice where there is no empathy, only the *survival of the fittest*. However, symbolic language cuts in all directions, not only do we know what it means to compete and dominate, we are able to conceive of loss and suffering. We *literally* live *through* others, evoking and invoking empathy.

Empathy therefore is the most logical, reasonable, and *ethical* basis for human life as *equal, significant,* and *Good* based in our common pre-symbolic nature, particularly if we believe that the self is literally a construction *of* others.

However, something occurs as the self becomes aware of its subjectivity. The self desires to be as unsubject as possible as there is an economy in nature of reward versus punishment which favors our will to power *over* subjectivity.

In the absence of a moral "God" it is by *nature* that humans are *not* created equal, but rather arise situationally as forces to be reckoned with. In this sense, we may conceive of how symbol-using adults may come to view innocent children of differing races and cultures *not* of equal significance or value.

However, such a view is contradictory, i.e., morality is very real, with very real consequences *between* humans. In fact more real than supernatural constructions, inasmuch as they cannot be logically connected to *reasonable* entities, particularly where said entities are wholly dependent upon *human language* and human *interpretation* in order to attain adherence.

It is *through* socially constructed *language* that individuals come to form beliefs regarding constructions of race, gender, and culture.

If all humans are *born* innocent, we necessarily become symbolically polluted *through* social constructions *of our own making.*

Socially constructed language *is* the medium *through* which we live and *become* (like fishes suspended in water). To presume that the absence of a *supernatural* entity gives one immunity from moral judgment is *literal* ignorance. One may escape the wrath of a supernatural God in an "afterlife," but one cannot escape the real-time social judgments of humans who are the arbiters of meaning.

One might suppose that the moral judgments of one's particular culture are the measure of *all* moral judgments. Such ethnocentric reasonings are the basis of moral constructions based within the supernatural and necessarily preclude socially constructed reality as *the* means of moral evolution.

If we were to agree that all *are* equal, significant, and Good based upon our common human nature and innocence of birth, *how* "significant" and "Good" *are* we and in relation to what? The moral construction that all are "equal" creates great tension in as far as we are *not*. Either we set about immediately redistributing value, i.e., resources, status, empathy, or we reconstruct our symbolic hypocrisy as "Good."

If we successfully redistributed value equally amongst all, thereby adhering to our dictum of equality based in the Good, questions arise, e.g., if we achieved an inherent quality of Good in humans through equal distribution of value, would not *more* humans equate to a still greater Good (as long as value was distributed equally)? Thus begging the question: *Who* should produce the additional offspring, and in what numbers?

If individual value is a function of first having been "created," then the manifest potential Power of *creating* is obscured and latently transferred to either a divine entity or a function of domination according to the laws of the Jungle.

The question of inherent individual Goodness opens a Pandora's box of inquiries in relation to what is the limit (if any) of human population in order to achieve the optimal Goodness, and if the optimal number of additional humans is a number less than that of an equally distributed ratio of offspring amongst contemporary couples, how do we decide which couples produce the additional offspring and which don't?

However, long before facing such conundrums, we would most likely grapple for considerable time with the difficulty of initially distributing equal value. One solution might be to terminate all human reproductive activity until such a time value had been equally distributed. *If* we place high value in all individuals, re-distribution of value should begin where it is most exigent and end where it is least so.

Once we had achieved such an exhausting process of redistribution of equal value, we might then set about to decide who reproduces and in what quantities. If *all* were not permitted to reproduce equally, we would re-encounter the conundrum of inequality. Here also, we come to more fully realize how technology subsumes biology.

Symbolic language functions to re-create our world according to dictums of value. If we decide that human life is of value, for example, our evolutionary trajectory becomes constrained within such constructions such that we can no longer merely reproduce at will according to natural instincts. All "natural" behavior is recast as meaningful *through language,* and like the perimeter fence surrounding a large refuge, we eventually run up against some symbolic construction which contains, constrains, or restricts our natural will.

If the earth can support only x amount of humans, then the "Goodness" ratio of human life is restricted by x (*unless* we turn to other *technological* solutions such as terraforming). Eventually, whether we are successful in the equal distribution of value or not, the earth's population will encounter a sustainable limit which will necessarily be subsumed within *technological* discourses. No longer does natural instinct, nor "manifest destiny," guide human evolution.

Inasmuch as we construct individuals (or anything) as *significant* yet fail to act positively upon such constructions, we create contradictions which engender collective guilt. The supernatural paradigm provides a scapegoat mechanism allowing us to transfer culpability, i.e., lay claim to the manifest Good while rejecting the latent evil, represented in the crushed bones of the vanquished upon which we build our ivory towers.

If we believed *explicitly* in the significance of *essential equality* between all humans or even those within local communities, a *tremendous* amount of activity in the direction of equality *is* possible, e.g., one might sell all of one's assets and redistribute (as equitably as possible) the value locally to those more in need. One then might donate as much time and labor as possible toward innumerable activities in service of equality. Short of this, even a marginal redistribution of *value* would be well within the range of possibilities.

Significance itself is a subjective and relative term. If we believe human life is *"significant,"* with which other subjective terms of value do we imbue it, and according to which standpoints? Wild animals ostensibly have a relatively fixed relationship with *sign*-ificance, i.e., food, security, reproduction, etc. For example, animals within a particular species typically consider food to consist of relatively stable and predictable components.

Significance for animals is likewise located within the individual (devoid of the self). The cries of a hungry chick are significant to its mother, however, the mother must first satiate *her* hunger in order to service the interests of her offspring.

Because language cuts in all directions, it is possible that such terms as "significance" and "value" can be dissected and reconstructed as a process of refining Truth in pursuit of the Good *through* language. Otherwise, terms are up for grabs, to be imbued with the meaning(s) of those with dominant voices.

Since human nature is essentially animal nature, our natural disposition toward significance is self-centered, e.g., the presymbolic infant is oriented toward its own needs. Not until we acquire language do we become aware of the needs of others. Later, the individual becomes aware of the greater needs of society as second-tier significance.

Individual animals (both human and nonhuman) instinctively know what is significant *to them* (whether they are hungry, thirsty, etc.). What is significant on a social level becomes more subjective as significance must necessarily be communicated *through* subjective symbolic meaning as opposed to empirical experience. Society is thus maintained through subjective and contradictory language.

If words *had* meaning as opposed to *conveying* meaning, and meaning was fixed across time, there wouldn't be significant need of communication as all would be known equally, independent of context. However, communication *is* the process of negotiating meaning across multiple ever-changing contexts since language is subjective and contextually conditioned, where community *is* the discursive paradigm of giving and acquiring voice.

The individual negotiates society symbolically in order to satiate *her/his* significant motives wherein language-induced "moral" contradictions instill guilt, shame, and embarrassment. The individual then seeks redemption by giving voice through association and alignment with like-minded organizational and ideological narratives of Good.

Since all individuals are made political by subjective language within the political paradigm, symbolic constraints are placed upon the individual, e.g., the social dictum of wearing clothes in the public. The individual evades guilt, shame, and embarrassment through compliance or resistance, e.g., association with a nudist colony, etc.

As an individual attempting to explore significance as a function of *human purpose* within the relative and subjective experience of social reality, this writer proposes the following paradigms as *significant* (toward annihilation of subjectivity), though not *necessarily* comprehensive nor in order of exigency:

Knowledge
Truth
Freedom
Liberty
Human Rights
Equality

As a *symbol-using* animal, the paradigm of knowledge is significant in relation to human purpose since *if* there is an ultimate destiny or *trajectory* toward which all human motive is drawn, then the only reasonable way to knowledge thereof it is *through* language.

Every human action (no matter how ostensibly remote) is made meaningful through subjective language. Meaning, i.e., "reality," is not "revealed" *by* language but is constructed *through* the technology *of* language, therefore every human action is a function of motive made meaningful, i.e., purposeful, through language.

Language circumscribes things and techniques as meaningful tools in the pursuit of Power over nature, e.g., through language, we learn to *acquire* resources which we then *control* and *synthesize* toward an ever greater *potentiality* in empowerment (Appendix I).

There's *nothing* passive in symbolic communication. Language *is* the process of symbolically ordering things in order to *control* them in pursuit of *Power over* subjectivity in nature *and* society. Symbolic language *is* technique, whereas knowledge of symbolic language *is* knowledge of technique, i.e., *technology*, i.e., knowledge *is Power.*

If anything *is* of significance, *it is language.* Language *is* significance. Language is the process of signifying all else, even the most abstract theories of physics and *human purpose.* All other "significances" live and die by knowledge (*or the lack thereof*) acquired through language. If *equality* of all humans is manifestly significant, then *equal knowledge* is the only logical basis upon which to construct it. Conversely, if equality of all is of less significance, we would expect to see a manifest hierarchical ordering of knowledge.

"*Truth*" is likewise a function of knowledge. We may speak of "Truth" and even discover "gravities" thereof with limited knowledge relative to a particular discursive context, however, due to subjective language, we always conclude some finer degree of greater knowledge is lacking, e.g., "I think, therefore I am." "I" am *what*? In relation to what? Some significant *description* detailing that which *"I" am not*?

Knowledge is fundamental to "Truth" even though knowledge itself is limited within the subjectivity of language. The highest manifestation of Truth is a function of the will to Good in balance with the will to Power (point a, Appendix V).

Freedom is a function of knowledge. As a linguistic construct, the concept of freedom as free of all subjectivity (resistance) is a fallacy. Animals in the wild may seem to be born free, however, they are fixed within a matrix of subjectivities, i.e., illness, injury, death, limited resources, time-space, etc. Animals are "free" in nature in so far as they are *empowered* in relation to their subjectivities.

Humans are bounded by corresponding subjectivities to nature in addition to subjectivities imposed by *symbolic language*. Within the political paradigm, knowledge *is* Power since the paradigm is a construct *of* knowledge (the highest point representing the "eye of gnosis"). Within nature *and* the symbolic paradigm of Power, Power has a reciprocal relationship to freedom. Power equals voice, and Power *over* equals *the ability to do otherwise* in relation to resistance, i.e., freedom.

Liberty is a function of knowledge, although perhaps more narrowly defined within the dialectic of agent versus subject. The mere existence of an agent versus subject dialectic is the manifestation of knowledge in the form of Power *over*. Depending on the definition, liberty does not denote the *absence* of resistance, but merely an ostensible absence of *oppressive* resistance.

If liberty is the freedom to pursue one's own best interests within a society without interfering with the interests of others, then liberty is only bounded by an individual's knowledge of what is possible and what constitutes "interference."

What is *possible* and what constitutes interference is elucidated through *acquired* knowledge. Human rights would ostensibly be of marginal significance if knowledge were shared *equally* since there would no longer exist a void of mystification (ignorance) within which to construct a basis of Power *over*, e.g., per the *Wonderful Wizard of Oz*.

Interestingly, one may infer a society's psychological orientation, and by extension, knowledge, through its *manifest* proclamations of significance, e.g., freedom, liberty, human rights, equality, etc., denote a proletarian orientation to *deficiency* in relation to Power.

In any case, significance originates in the pre-symbolic *individual* as positive and negative sensory stimuli, while symbolic significance arises as the individual is inducted into the symbolic paradigm of Power.

Although individuals may chose to circumscribe differing sets of subject matter as "significant" according to differing standpoints, we conclude that whatever is chosen as significant has a direct and corollary relationship with actual and *perceived* subjectivities of the individual within a greater cultural domain of social subjectivities within the existential realm of subjectivity.

Subjectivity reigns down from on high in the political paradigm, as "hot potatoes" subsuming the individual. Individuals clamor and claw their way up the Pyramid of Power in order to escape the subjectivities of nature *and* of one another.

As we rise in the hierarchy, we eagerly discharge a quantum of subjectivity down upon those lower in the hierarchy who likewise discharge it to those still lower, etc.

If humans are manifestly moral beings of divine nature, *and/or* our language allows us to imagine and construct a *manifestly* moral, fair, and Good reality, and *if* in fact our presumption of society *is* that of a manifestly moral and Good society, then it is the duty of each individual to ensure Goodness through the exchange of knowledge through proactive giving and acquiring of *critical voice.*

Society (community) consists in a collective net will based upon the sexual paradigm from which it arises. It is the subject position (standpoint) of the individual suspended within the social web of meaning which is most significant in analyzing, identifying, and reconstructing the Good of society according to *reasoned* arguments through the giving and acquiring of *critical* voice in resistance to manifest (and latent) Power *over relationships.*

Culture

Since there is no natural way of being in the world, language organizes and mediates all human activity. Although the family is the most fundamental and organic social structure, there is no manner in which it can be organized independent of *symbolic* meaning.

Due to the primacy of the sexual paradigm of Power, couplings and families will manifest themselves regardless of cultural orientation, however, symbolic language *is* the social process which serves to align common values within distinctive discursive communities, e.g., hunting, gathering, agrarian, etc. Therefore, the values around which symbolic meanings are constructed is reflected in the nature of subsequent meanings such as "family," or any significant term within a particular cultural orientation, e.g., capitalism, socialism, etc.

Everything is relative, particularly human *culture*. The evolution of human culture is analogous to our Hierarchy of Motives (Appendix IV) in that diverse cultures tend to share similar values based in the more basic motives, i.e., *biological* and increasingly dissimilar values as they evolve toward motives of *potentiality*. Likewise, our Hierarchy of Motives is analogous to the evolution of the human mind from instinctual to the conceptual.

As cultures evolve, values which are rooted in instinctual, *biological* motives become sophisticated and complex as they evolve toward the conceptual since symbolic language allows for infinite and increasingly complex constructions of meaning.

As cultural constructions of meaning evolve, they become canonized within supernatural narratives unique to a particular cultural orientation. Such narratives serve to unify and give meaningful purpose to each culture, thereby authenticating each culture's technological achievement *as Good.*

Culture is analogous to Freud's *ego* inasmuch as it mediates between the animalistic desires of the individual as the *id* and the greater society as the *superego.* As we develop from infancy, our animalistic desires of the sexual paradigm are reined in and regulated by what is deemed socially acceptable within the highest conceptions of symbolic language. The result being moralized local cultures within which the individual acts.

Viewed as the "ego," culture represents a paradigm of tension between biology and technology wherein technology, i.e., symbolic language, necessarily subsumes our biological orientation. Since subjectivity to nature is viewed as greater than subjectivity to symbolic language, we gravitate toward the Power of technology *over* nature.

Within any given cultural paradigm, individuals *continuously* struggle over the definition of meaning, e.g., a particular culture may utilize a flag as one of its dominant unifying symbols (although *all* symbols are subjective, including words), and each will seek to imbue it with meanings with which each is most intimately vested, e.g., capitalism, nationalism, imperialism, patriotism, democracy, family values, etc.

Culture therefore is the net effect of a dialectical struggle over "meaning." Ultimately, net culture (as it is recognized) favors the *dominant* voices within a given community in the same manner as history (*his story*) is recorded by its victors. Thus, both dominate culture and history *manifestly* represent a particular and privileged worldview.

Enculturation, thus, is a profound socializing force since humans are linguistic animals which are socially constructed and subject to social judgment, i.e., pollution/purification. Within more or less collectivist/egalitarian cultures, one should expect to find less contention and stratification over symbolic meaning, thus forming a Pyramid of Power with a relatively gradual gradient and less disparity between the dominant and subservient classes. Conversely, within a more individualistic/competitive culture, one should expect to find continual contention and profound stratification as individuals compete for dominance over a profusion of meanings.

Since technology subsumes biology, there is *no* escaping meaning. As symbol-using animals, we must necessarily align ourselves *one way or another* within *meaningful* relationships. Everything we do and say, the way we dress, the people with whom we associate, the contexts within which we "find" ourselves, bespeak a particular cultural orientation, *some* of which is consciously chosen, but most of which is enacted *unconsciously*.

Since *all* meaning is merely a construction which favors a particular worldview, meaning also serves to *resist* competing worldviews, e.g., the term "created" promotes a cultural view that all men are equal by *divine nature*. Within such a term, "equality" is a function of the *individual* will to (moral) "Good" and not hegemonic culture.

Culture is by definition, "organic," similar to something which grows out of something else. That "something else" is our evolutionary nature. Animals cannot be said to have culture, merely instinct and natural behavior.

However, with the advent of symbolic language, we are able to "cultivate" meaning over and above nature. In order to cultivate meaning, we must first give voice, i.e., circumscribe something as socially significant. The act of giving voice is *not* a neutral event, but rather an act of will with the possibility of both positive and negative consequences, just as animal acts are acts of will with consequences (aggression/submission).

In the absence of other knowledge, we must necessarily assume a commonsense orientation to significance in order to *endeavor* to achieve consubstantiation with an unknown audience. This process of enculturation is observable whenever a group of unfamiliar individuals is assembled within a context, such as the first day of class in an institution of learning.

For example, within the above context requiring a moderator (professor), and the prolonged absence thereof, even though it is not officially required, someone will inevitably *give voice* to something of ostensible (common) significance, e.g., utilizing a contextually *assumed* language, someone will circumscribe the professor's tardiness in relation to the shared context, or the weather, or any perceived anecdote of *significance*, since all social context is meaningful and continuously requires elucidative sense-making.

It is in this manner, culture is circumscribed and given form through the force of *will* in giving voice to that which is *assumed* by the speaker to be of significance (common) to his or her audience. Ninety-nine percent of anything is just *showing up* (giving voice). Ninety-eight percent of this is showing up *first* and leaving *last*.

Culture is built upon commonsense assumptions, i.e., easily recognizable and meaningful *action routines* within simple contexts of meaning, e.g., hunter-gatherer or early agrarian societies, etc. Common-sense making, as commonly understood and elucidated *action-routines*, i.e., what anyone is commonly understood to be doing within a given context, *is* the basis of culture.

Low-tech cultures, i.e., hunter-gatherer, agrarian, nomadic, etc., rely upon commonly understood meanings in order to function efficiently within such cultures based in substance, i.e., commodities, tools, labor. High-tech cultures can no longer afford to rely upon an assumptive and taken-for-granted epistemic method of sense-making in a world of symbolic *forms* (where everything is founded upon *form*al agreements).

Thomas Paine's *Common Sense* couldn't possibly be as effectual today as during the Enlightenment era of 1776 due to demassification and technology. Unifying ideals such as manifest destiny and divine providence together with fewer channels of communication allowed for the dissemination of information to a receptive mass audience oriented in a more *common* approach to reason. That which may have appeared overtly and singularly oppressive in 1776 has become covert, multifarious, and nebulous.

In a postmodern Godless society, "Truth" is up for grabs and filtered through multiple channels of (vested) interest. There was a time when a man or woman could have cried, "wolf," and the townspeople would have responded with pitchforks in hand. Today, the "wolf" has dissolved into the cyber-forest, and the people subsumed and delusional have returned home to their Xboxes.

In an uncommon-sense (postmodern) society, Truth *can* be found in Power, i.e., one may not discover fundamental "moral" Truths nor Gods, nor demons, however one consistently discovers a manifest structure of Power *over* within the hegemony.

While postmodern culture is skeptical of fundamental Truths, it is intensely interested in defining existential "Truths" of its own. If said Truths are *empowering,* further refinement is resisted (ignored) if it undermines empowerment, as per the "Emperor's New Clothes."

All cultures, modern, postmodern, etc., exist within frameworks of Power and serve to both sustain and resist Power in their movements (social cohesiveness is a Powerful motive of its own within the greater Power structure). It is in the best interest of the Powerful that the people believe in the "Emperor's New Clothes" and the authority which they represent.

Similar to the *Wonderful Wizard of Oz,* Power works to create illusions of reality in the form of belief through its ubiquitous and nebulous channels of propaganda through which it aligns itself with popular culture. In this manner, the people surreptitiously become emotionally vested in a belief in the emperor's clothes through complicity with popular culture.

Let us *briefly* consider a few common contradictory paradigms of cultural (socially constructed) reality from an uncommon-sense perspective: if the highest manifest Truth of family is based on the Good of humanity, all reproductive activities would cease together with all exclusive relationships until the entire world became an equal sharing "family" unto itself in order to ensure the manifest Good among all equally. If the social construction "family" is manifestly based in the motive of moral "Goodness" we should not expect to observe couples forming *exclusive* relationships and having children as though an afterthought, without giving voice or consideration to any current state of inequality.

Commonsense-making involves tradition and abstraction as its epistemology such that the more an individual searches for Truth, "reality" dissovles into the mystical world beyond the culpability of humans. One may thus reason that the Good of the entire world is beyond one's control, therefore, if one conforms to the dictums of one's own culture, one is purified in the eyes of God.

A commonsense approach to reasoning allows one to invert the telescope, thereby circumscribing microcosms of reality as though everything were separate and distinguished as opposed to the view that everything is connected and continuous.

If we examine the whole of evolution and humans as products of evolution rather than undefined divine powers, it makes absolute sense that humans couple exclusively *and* seek public sanction *and* reproduce with little to no thought of the overall Good of humanity.

Our animal ancestors competitively mated and reproduced since it is through successful reproduction that they avoid extinction and survived to evolve. The highest Good of our ancestors was the survival of the fittest *individuals*, not species. Each individual looks after its own interest first, then that of its mate and offspring. This is the Power of the sexual paradigm just as rising in the hierarchy is the Power of the political paradigm.

Sustenance

The closest approximation to what may have consisted of a natural diet for pre-symbolic humans might be found within wild chimpanzees. Short of this, whatever is considered "food" is culturally relative.

"Food" must necessarily consist, first, in what is available. Since we have populated nearly every continent on earth, what is available varies widely. Essentially, anything we can metabolize which gives us more energy than is required to acquire and synthesize could be food.

At the same time we are naming food through symbolic language, we are naming all else surrounding us as more or less "Good" or "evil." If we have reasons to fear or be suspicious of a thing such as a snake, we may label it as "evil," therefore, when considered as food, we likely will also consider it "evil," and therefore aesthetically unpalatable (even though it may in fact be a widely available and nutritious food source). Where what is available is abundant and diverse, many constructions of *food* may occur across many varying cultural perceptions of "Good" versus "evil." Thus whatever "food" is, is merely a cultural (social) construction as is *how* it's prepared, stored, eaten, etc.

Food necessarily comes from nature as an evolutionary process, therefore that which is readily available in nature and provides sufficient energy and nutrition to justify its acquisition is ostensibly the most natural and beneficial food for the human body.

As food becomes commodified, its manifest value as essential health and nutrition to the body becomes a latent motive while its profit value becomes the manifest motive. Therefore, genetic monoculture in favor of the highest profit margins supplants the evolutionary benefits of natural genetic diversity.

The will to Power over drives markets such that production is compelled to extremes of competition. Commercial farming outstrips natural cycles (as technology subsumes nature) such that petroleum-based amendments *must* be added to the soil in order to produce sustainable commercial volumes of commodities.

Such adulterated commodities are then exploited innumerable ways in order to maximize profitability, e.g., processed, repackaged, chemically altered, amended, remade into more costly and appealing products.

Food becomes so commodified that it becomes normalized to go to a grocery store for food without any concept of hunting, killing, butchering, sowing, reaping, harvesting, or preserving. Commodities which individuals once produced for themselves are typically arranged around the perimeter of a store while the more highly profitable, packaged, and processed products must be passed by or through near the center. Placid music aids toward recasting the process of acquiring food into an aesthetically pleasing experience.

Meanwhile, a ubiquitous array of restaurants and fast-food enterprises await just outside. These commercial establishments exist to manifestly profit from convenience and aesthetics as opposed to health, nutrition, or thrift. Convenience stores dilute nutrition further by promoting a stunning array of sugars, carbohydrates, and items of vice at inflated prices.

Food is no longer acquired and consumed as an essential fuel of the active body but as a recreational aesthetic novelty of gratification. Fast- "food" is *engineered* to be aesthetically gratifying as opposed to nutritious, e.g., copious amounts of fat, carbohydrates, salts, sugars, and artificial flavorings.

A commonsense view of popular fast-food establishments would seem to consist in them as aesthetically pleasing oases of capitalistic virtue, i.e., "progress," where one can acquire quality, gratifying food conveniently and economically.

An uncommon-sense view of popular fast-food establishments might consist in a view of them as corporations of cultural mass production for profit which utilize mass-produced, genetically altered, chemically amended, and mechanically raised and processed, animals, animal by-products, and monocrop agriculture.

However, larger fast-food corporations are not in the business of "fast food" per se, but rather in the business of *leveraging assets*, i.e., real estate. Just as in the game of Monopoly, land is acquired according to knowledge of population growth patterns and public works projects as a potentially profitable investment. A restaurant is constructed and leased to a franchisee who makes payments on the mortgage while the corporation realizes the growing equity of the real estate which is used to capitalize more franchises.

In essence, the common-sense-making fast food devotee pays incredibly inflated prices for mass-produced, unhealthy "food" prepared by strangers from the (culturally recognized) lower echelons of the labor pool in order to support the growth and expansion of superficial, plastic "playlands" and ultimately large corporations which usurp substance (in the form of real estate, *the ultimate source of wealth and Power*), while impoverishing themselves through the use of inflating fiat monies, thereby becoming ever more detached from the wealth of substance, i.e., of the *land* and evermore reliance upon corporate "convenience."

What constitutes "food" and its interrelationship with cultural norms as false consciousness in relation to human purpose could fill volumes, therefore, we condense but a sampling of its interconnectivity, i.e., technology subsumes nature, big money supports big oil, big oil supports mass production, which supports commercialism, which supports private corporations, which acquire public benefits, which monopolize substantive Power over the people.

In Western society, we are obsessed with diet and weight loss. This phenomenon is a manifest sign of many contradictions, i.e., unnatural diet as opposed to a healthy diet, unnatural physical activity as opposed to being physically active, gluttonousness as opposed to charitableness, medicalization as opposed to natural health, consumerism as opposed to self-reliance.

Unhealthy food and an inability to produce healthy food supports a medical-industrial complex which supports private corporations which provide convenience to the masses in exchange for land, substance, Power and economic independence.

What is culturally constructed as food is not a result of a manifest will to the Good, but rather a manifest will to profit and control, i.e., a manifest will to Power *over*.

Drugs/Vice

Drugs and alcohol serve to mask the many latent social contradictions such as food and its latent effects, i.e., cancer, diabetes, cardiovascular disease, etc., and innumerable social ills brought about by contradictions in values.

We are just as addicted to drugs and alcohol in our postmodern world as we are to convenience and fast food, all of which our ancestors did without for thousands of years. All drugs, alcohol, and vice have latent (side) effects as all circumscribe some manifest Good while de-accentuating the bad. As one popular song lyric puts it: "You don't get something for nothing. You can't have freedom for free."

Many drugs are likewise based in petrochemicals and create additional revenue for law firms as latent side effects become manifest health concerns. Conversely, more natural substances such as marijuana have relatively fewer and less serious latent effects but are highly regulated since as a commercial crop, it would decrease and even replace (in a truly environmentally concerned world) many petroleum-based industries.

There is no logical correlation between a substance, how dangerous it is to individuals, and its "illegality," i.e., alcohol is more addictive and has potentially more serious side effects than many "illegal" substances. For the commonsense thinker, it's easy to forget that world history would be immeasurably altered if hemp had been illegal. A tremendous amount of commerce and discovery would not have occurred without the sails of ships which were made of hemp. The U.S. Declaration of Independence, Constitution, and Bill of Rights were all written on hemp paper.

The (slightly) underground torrent of pornography is testament to social psychosis brought on by social engineering and the resultant guilt, shame and embarrassment associated with the human body and its functions. Alternatively, just as with any other vice, a tremendous amount of revenue is generated for Media corporations in this ubiquitous, technology-driving medium.

Whatever is deemed an illegal substance, or vice, is not manifestly so deemed for the protection of the individual. They are so deemed for control over the individual according to Powerful commercial interests.

Clothing

If there is anything which attests to our axiom that there is no longer any natural way of being in the world, it is the nearly universal dictum of clothes-wearing in public.

Even though culture is a most profound and primal social condition, like fish suspended in water, it is the last thing we notice. From an evolutionary standpoint, clothes-wearing makes sense, e.g., if we in fact arose from the sexual paradigm, the first thing to be contested within the political paradigm would be reproductive rights. These could either be determined and regulated by the law of the jungle or by symbolic imperatives. Therefore, technological language subsumed the natural biological promiscuity and aggressiveness of nature within the mandate of clothes-wearing.

The profound socializing Power of culture is exemplified in clothes-wearing. Even criminals and members of countercultures conform to clothes-wearing. Just as clothes-wearing is a subjective social construction which is typically taken for granted, so too are a host of other subjective social assumptions which are implicated in Power relationships, e.g., if one is expected to wear clothes in public, then one must necessarily be expected to have *some* form of social resources in order to obtain clothes, i.e., gainful employment, friends, relatives, etc.

Ignorance and lack of social resources creates an instructor/student hierarchy as the socially uninformed becomes instructed as to proper social etiquette. In the absence of sufficient resources, one might fashion "clothing" out of skins or leaves, however, in absence of alternative contexts, one thus adorned will be restricted to a social role relevant to the aesthetic standards of the local culture, i.e., lunatic. Within symbolic social culture, clothes (and language) truly make the man, and woman, particularly insofar as the woman's *body* is circumscribed as *predominantly* significant. Clothes as symbols are hollow signifiers which are imbued with ever-changing hegemonic and cultural meanings.

From a creationist viewpoint, the human body is deemed to be sinful due to disobedience and duality in the knowledge of Good *and* evil, thus the "natural" corruptible man must cover his shame (duality) in a morally conscious world. From an evolutionary viewpoint, clothes-wearing is a sign of technology subsuming nature in a continuous transmutation away from the subjectivity of nature (law of the jungle), toward knowledge in the *Power over nature.*

Entertainment

To "entertain" is to contain within, i.e., to voice an idea or concept which subsumes the mind and keeps it focused through fascination. One may focus another's attention purely for the enjoyment of the other, but even here, the entertainer himself/herself, seeks to control or acquire some beneficial relationship.

Entertainment occurs within a context containing latent motives. It occurs organically as a tribe or clan retells the events of the day through stories, songs, and rituals which serve to fortify the common values and meaning of the day's activities. The *manifest* festival has the *latent* effect of social cohesion. One should wonder as to the larger contexts in which entertainment is being provided. Nothing is free, therefore, if a corporation or state is providing "playlands" or constructing magnificent public works, one should become curious as to the *latent* motives thereof together with all possible implications, e.g., as per the dog, Toto, in the *Wonderful Wizard of Oz*.

"Plays, farces, spectacles, gladiators, strange beasts, medals, pictures and other such opiates were for ancient peoples the bait toward slavery, the price of their liberty, the instruments of tyranny" (Etienne de La Boétie).

If one believes in the divine right of kings, one might naively suppose that such benevolent and divinely guided leaders would seek to entertain their subjects purely out of a divine will to Good.

186

However, everything bears a cost, even *bread and circus*. One might ask *how* such costs are met and what the *actual* costs in fact are.

Where divine right is lacking, even street corner performers expect *something* in return for entertaining. Entertainment thus becomes a *hollow signifier* which can delight, amuse, educate, or *deceive* (*caveat emptor*). A culture starving for entertainment is a culture subsumed.

Within *manifest* slavery, culture and entertainment assumes the forms of *resistance* and *rejoinder*. The *overtly* oppressive condition of manifest slavery gives rise to creative expressions of discontent and resistance.

Within *latent* slavery, i.e., under the *iron*, as opposed to *wooden* yoke of slavery, the masses are so *covertly* subsumed within an illusion and false consciousness that they believe themselves not only to *be* free, but *extraordinarily so* within an inverted reality such that a citizen-laborer conceives of himself as a sovereign-entrepreneur and the entertainer a champion of his Goodness.

Popular entertainment serves to patronize and pacify the masses within latent slavery. The Powerful entertainment corporations serve as gatekeepers in deciding what is popular entertainment through a multiplicity of channels of influence, thereby reifying the status quo.

Although a relatively small subliminal underground movement of "slave-conscious" entertainment exists, it becomes diluted, commercialized, and repackaged as "mainstream" culture, e.g., in as far as "rap" music was initially intended as a method of *giving and acquiring critical voice* from a socially disadvantaged standpoint, i.e., as *rapport*, it has also been subsumed within popular culture, for the sake of entertainment.

Culture is a hollow signifier which often *forgets* that which was initially signified. What was initially signified was often based in substance, i.e., a popular song which initially conveyed the meaning of redemption and forgiveness may become subsequently imbued with alternate meanings and eventually reduced to a "ribbon" symbolizing solidarity in war or any number of special interests.

The *tattoo* as art and social expression, has likewise been subsumed within popular culture. What was once more or less an expression of counterculture or identification with a distinctive group or status has become a sign of cultural and demographic identity, as though a postmodern expression of expressing for the sake of expression.

Interestingly, if we compare the contemporary phenomenon of tattooing with the graffiti of the late 1960s as a counterculture movement giving critical voice in opposition to governments and mainstream society, as symbolic of the reclamation of public spaces and ownership by the people who inhabited them, then tattooing as a countercultural movement makes sense within *latent* slavery as the collective consciousness of the enslaved attempts to demarcate itself as the last bastion of freedom, and therefore control, in an unfree world (as symbol users and abusers).

At some point, art must imitate life as art is meaningless without subjective language, and symbolic language *is* the process of naming things as Good or evil, *relative to humans.* Therefore, art as entertainment and entertainment as art necessarily gives *creative* voice, or serves to obfuscate, a particular worldview or views. No communication is neutral since we are *meaningful* subjects suspended within a matrix of subjectivities. All communication serves to empower *someone* in relation to subjectivity. Entertainment is merely another form of *giving voice* as an expression of our will to Good and Power over subjectivity.

The Automobile

Of unique cultural and technological significance is the automobile. It represents both an objective and analogous expression of psychological motivation. Neither an automobile nor a motorist would move without psychological *motivation,* and all psychological motivation is arguably implicated within *some* physical action (motion), such as operating a motor vehicle.

In relation to human motivation, communication, and individual will, the motorist, together with the automobile within the context of the rules of the road, presents an exceptional real-time laboratory for examining human motive within a context of meaning.

From a technological standpoint, the cultural-automotive paradigm presents a stark example of how technology subsumes nature, for example, it is difficult to imagine anyone alive today whose subjectivity has not been reduced or in some manner altered by the automobile. As ambulatory devices, human legs and feet cannot compete with automotive technology.

Although an individual could altogether eschew the automobile, she or he could not compete economically nor socially within contemporary western society in the absence of some alternate form of *technology*. There simply is no way of avoiding technology *nor its implications within human subjectivity.* An individual *could* survive in the wilderness in a very low-tech environment, but not a *no-tech* environment since the knowledge of the technique of *language* itself is irrevocably implicated within all human action.

Although no one can absolutely ascertain a given motive merely by an observed behavior, human behavior within a controlled context may be analyzed as either more or less True or false across a Truth-refining dialectic, thereby revealing general patterns of behavior which may be implicated in motive.

If we first imagine automobiles driven by robots (computers) as our control group in comparison of human behavior, we would expect a robot motorist to behave efficiently and logically with respect to other robot motorists (assuming they were so programmed). If robot motorists communicated electronically such that each continuously monitored and adjusted its behavior so as to function at optimal efficiency and minimal damage, we should *not* expect any damage to occur, and we *would* expect conformity to the rules of the road and the use of infrastructures as intended.

If we consider velocity as a controlling parameter of behavior such that certain thoroughfares were restricted in both maximum and minimum speeds, we should expect our robot subjects to maintain speeds within those parameters which were most efficient and safe between them. However, since "purpose" is missing within our control group, we would need to factor in "maximum speed" as equal to "highest efficiency."

From this writer's standpoint, at nearly any given point in time, one may enter a thoroughfare as a passenger or motorist and witness a *majority* of (human) motorists which do not conform to the posted speed limits (usually at the maximum parameter). *If* this is true, and even if it is closer to one in one hundred, it becomes a sign of meaning *outside* of any motive contained within the prescribed speed limits.

Since no human behavior occurs outside of meaning, any meaning of an alternate speed can be analyzed in terms of individual motive. If a (human) motorist were to claim that he or she merely wasn't monitoring his or her speed *momentarily* and therefore crept *a little* over (or under) the limit, this *indicates* some alternate dominating motive other than that of monitoring one's speed. If it were mandated that all motorists' (human and robot) vehicles self-destructed upon breaching the prescribed speed limits, it seems likely that human motorists would monitor their speed such that they would stay well within the prescribed limits just as the robots.

The above example, if true, implicates an individual will to Power *over* socially agreed parameters, i.e., whatever else is of motivational concern to a given individual is *allowed* to dominate over her or his motives of social cohesiveness. If it were a categorical imperative that motorists conform to speed limits or be penalized instantaneously though a GPS points system covertly, an ostensibly massive number of motorists would lose their "privilege" to drive. Thus exemplifying our axiom of biological subsummation *by* technology.

However, human motives are extremely complex, motorists are subject to an extensive and multifarious hierarchy of motives, e.g., an emergency may arise wherein an individual requires transport to a medical facility as quickly as possible. Under such conditions, it is likely that the motorist may not be penalized because of the context of the infraction. However, this too exemplifies technology subsuming nature since due to our human *subjectivity,* we *cannot* conform *absolutely* to the rigors of technological exactitude.

If we discount those motorists with reasonable motives, we are still left with a veritable plethora of alternative motives in terms of violators. Any proposed excuse for violation must somehow implicate some Power *over* relationship, i.e., being late for work implicates a motive of timeliness as dominant over the motive to comply. Therefore, the individual's *personal* motive of being a "reliable employee" is allowed to dominate *over* the motive of conforming to a *social* contract.

Although it is often difficult to isolate and interpret human motive in bodily action within the random *interpersonal* interplay in public places, the automobile, within the context of the rules of the road, filters out subjective human behaviors while circumscribing objective and mechanistic motions.

Within our robot scenario, it would be illogical and counterintuitive to program robots or engineer vehicles or infrastructures so as to disrupt efficiency or risk collateral damage. Likewise, it would seem within our human scenario—this is not to assume that all vehicles and infrastructures are engineered without imperfection, but rather, that such common basic standards may be used as a yardstick against which to measure behaviors in action.

Nearly any behavior can be analyzed and measured in relation to established and agreed upon standards, therefore there are innumerable variables beyond that of speed which may be analyzed. From a *communicative* perspective, the use (or non-use) of illuminated signaling devices is of special significance.

Within our robot scenario, perhaps visual signals would be replaced by a system of digital signals which alert oncoming robots of the impending maneuvers of others, and vice versa. In such a scenario, each robot would *absolutely* be dependent upon acquiring and responding to the signals of others.

If the use of signals (communication) was implicated in a social agreement and if in fact a motorist made such an explicit or implied agreement, then non-use constitutes a latent motive of individual will to Power *over* other motorists and those with whom said individual formed such agreements.

The ostensible, ubiquitous, inconsistent/non-use of signals amongst motorists puts into stark relief a veritable plethora of possible human motives all of which are ostensibly based within a will to Power apart from, and or Power over, other motorists and by extension, social contracts.

One may never know another's intention *absolutely,* particularly in a world of subjectivities, e.g., a signal indicator may have malfunctioned or some other systemic failure may have occurred. However, *intention* is a function of responsibility, and responsibility *is* what is required within subjectivity, i.e., one should always be ready, willing, and able to *respond* to the subjectivities of life, *if* anything matters.

If one *had* intended to communicate (signal) as per *agreement* and as per logic of *safety,* according to a motive of Power *with,* one then might have been *more* wary of any indication of malfunction and would likewise routinely inspect a vehicle prior to operating it.

From within a commonsense perspective, many things may appear insignificant, trivial, and unrelated. From within an uncommon-sense perspective, everything is connected within a language-based technological paradigm of Power which is constructed upon systems of knowledge which have increasingly less room for error and become exponentially complex over time.

Within contemporary culture, where the precision of technology determines our destiny, and we are eagerly subsumed, we become lulled into a stupor of colloquial ignorance in our cultural understanding of its full implications. Communication *is* the process of community, culture, and *sense-making*. The automobile provides an artificial cocoon as latent Power apart from response-ability to others.

Society

As Burke has suggested, *"Man is the symbol-using and abusing animal, inventor of the negative, separated from his natural condition by instruments of his own making, goaded by the spirit of hierarchy, and rotten with perfection."*

As human beings, we are socialized through the process of communication wherein the aggregate of human society is held together and controlled through the structure of community. It is the invention of the symbolic which allows us to *discriminate* between the Good and the "evil," thereby structuring society hierarchically.

Social Structure is analogous to a galaxy wherein gravitational forces between bodies are analogous to communication and community to the overall gravitational structure of a galaxy. The presence of a black hole at its center is not dissimilar to a region of *unsubjectivity*. In this model, Power is greatest at the center of the galaxy where ultimate culmination of perfection is attained within the black hole as *annihilation of all subjectivity, i.e.,* resistance.

We can neither predict nor know the True nature of unsubjectivity since we are necessarily restricted within the *oppositional* domain of symbolic language. However, we can predict the eventual annihilation of subjectivity in the absence of other knowledge, since as long as language serves to purify meaning, and Power to reduce subjectivity, there is ostensibly no other *reasonable* or *logical* conclusion other than eventual annihilation of subjectivity.

Passing from this life into whatever "reality" may consist of may in fact constitute unsubjectivity in the absence of symbolic meaning wherein we "devolve through multidimensional" realms which culminate within a singularity. Interestingly, even those of who are subscribe to a lesser fate such as a "paradise" or "heaven"—necessarily based in opposition—do not seem particularly *eager* to get there.

Meanwhile, the unknowable nature of unsubjectivity coupled with our reality based in oppositional meaning leaves us *manifestly* groping for Power within subjectivity while *latently* rushing headlong toward *unsubjectivity*. We are *even now* so subsumed within our "Precambrian" epoch of symbolic evolution that we as yet could care less about actual annihilation of subjectivity.

What we *are* obsessed with is Power within the seemingly endless bounds of our own subjectivity. Therefore, the brightest stars near the center of our social galaxy consist of the more Powerful across various dialectics of sexual, social, economic, and symbolic paradigms. The less Powerful languor on the outer fringes of the social galaxy, and just beyond, the evolutionary dusts from which we were formed.

As orbital bodies within our social galaxy, we symbolically gravitate toward unsubjectivity, i.e., a tremendous amount of social interplay occurs as we symbolically negotiate our individual subjectivities one with another. Our subjectivity begins with our *cultural* location at birth within our local galaxies from which we obtain our knowledge in symbolic sense-making, thus giving us a belief system within our localized cluster. Armed with said beliefs, we discriminate between differing clusters and beliefs within our galaxy in making choices pursuant of actions in our quest for unsubjectivity.

Evolution of technology intensifies nearer the center of our social galaxy where a tremendous amount of gravitational interplay occurs in the exchange of *voice*, i.e., ideas, information, *knowledge*. Knowledge is Power, thus gravitational attraction increases near the center, thus drawing in, yet, greater numbers of bodies seeking escape from subjectivity.

Within this model, Power is not distributed, but accreted. It is the lure of *the Good* (of unsubjectivity) which draws bodies inward, shifting the center of the gravity of Power in favor of those already empowered. Those already empowered become increasingly so due to cultural positioning in space-time. Power is accreted from the extremities in pursuit of annihilation.

In Sum

If anything matters, it can only be elucidated and scrutinized through symbolic, language. *If* all human action is ultimately rooted within motives of *unsubjectivity*, then it *is* significant to consider all human action *as* symbolic action in pursuit of potential Power *over* subjectivity, since we compete over resources in the pursuit thereof.

If all human action *is* essentially symbolic acquisition of potential Power over subjectivity, and *if* all "men" are either *created* or through symbolic action, *deemed* to be *equal*, then *all* human *action* should be scrutinized as *significant* to the *equal* Goodness of all.

There *may* in fact be divine force(s) responsible for all of creation, however, the only way we can become knowledgeable of and unified under such force(s) is *through* language.

Our extensive search for divine meaning through subjective language has produced a *veritable plethora* of Gods and demons spanning the entirety of human history. Such beings and narratives remain elusive to reason *except* when one (*through reason*) considers them as rhetorical machinations for the purpose of controlling the minds of the masses—*then* their Truth and purpose becomes manifestly revealed.

If all men are neither divinely nor symbolically created *equal* according to dominant contemporary narratives, *but wish to be*, each should arise and explicitly give *critical voice* according to each individual standpoint as a process of refining the highest Truth as a manifestation of Power *with*.

If it should turn out that equality *does* matter, such that individuals are motivated to arise and give critical voice, *knowledge* must be *acquired* and *shared* since one cannot critique that of which one is ignorant. Knowledge *is* Power, however Power is useless without the Good. If the Good consists in Power *with* as opposed to manifest Power *over relationships*, we should seek to *resist* technologies which increase Power *over*, and instead seek technologies which increase Power *with*, as a balance between our *will to Power over* and *will to Good* as our highest manifestation of Truth. *If* inequality and Power *over* are deemed *unjust*, then there could be *no* evil in critical analysis nor resistance thereto.

If reality *is* a social construction, then we each give "voice" to any particular construction thereof through everything we think, say, and do, thereby supporting, resisting, or reconstructing the status quo. *If* everything we think, say, and do either supports or resists the status quo, yet we do not believe or even *suspect* that our reality is as Good as it ought to be, then it is incumbent upon every individual to critically scrutinize and resist those things which appear unjust or unreasonable and support the just and reasonable.

If Subjective Annihilation Theory provides a *theoretical* basis for critically analyzing human action as a function of (*actual*) subjectivity, and if we can discover a reasonable common *Good* as the basis for human equality, then we at minimum have constructed a framework within which to *begin* discourses concerning human purpose as a function of our collective manifest Good.

The technology of the Internet is most a propos in terms of beginning to give and acquire voice. *No revolution nor technology in the history of the world has had as much potential for peacefully emancipating the Good of humanity at the level of the individual.* If we genuinely desire equality and Good for every individual and believe that each of us are a *product of society*, then the technology of the Internet in conjunction with its autonomous open-source technologies is a fertile ground for a profound reengineering of human destiny.

New knowledge in pursuit of our *will to Good* begins with new approaches to *supporting* and or *resisting* meaning at the level of the *individual* and *society*. The pale blue dot we have named Earth is *a bounty of resources,* if shared *intelligently* and *equally.*

Our search for human purpose through the lens of evolution as the mechanism of creation reveals a cohesive and logical theory of human purpose as a function of our natural desire to overcome subjectivity. In nature it is our will to Power *over* subjectivity and survival of the fittest in the pursuit thereof which is our dominating motive as opposed to moral "Goodness."

However, even if we consider human motives through the lens of mysticism as per creationism, we must *logically* conclude that the will to Power *over* is our dominating motive, as even herein remains a hierarchy of Power *over*, i.e., God as all-Powerful (a logical paradox) within an hierarchy of saints and sinners.

Our evolutionary nature is oriented in attending to the needs and desires of the *self.* However *language* allows us to recreate reality apart from nature such that we can conceive of social constructs such as equality, fairness, justice, etc.

So powerful is symbolic communication that within one sentence we can lay waste to millions of years of evolution, competition, and dominance, and throw down the gauntlet of morality declaring; *"from this moment forward let all pursue the manifest motive that all are equal in our collective quest for unsubjectivity."*

However language caused guilt exists in dialectical tension with *evolutionary* advantage where those in a superior position of Power naturally seek to retain individual advantage since relinquishing Power in the name of the "Good" of the other has the net effect of increasing the subjectivity of the *self* while correspondingly reducing access to the Good of the *self.*

Whether or not this essay is sufficient as a collection of ideas relating to human purpose or merely as a gadfly for the purpose of stimulating significant discourses relating to human purpose, the tension between the individual will to the Good of nature and language caused moral guilt will continue unabated as we endlessly claw our way towards unsubjectivity. The (supernatural) scape goat mechanism will likewise continue to work to deflect culpability away from ourselves and into the lap of the Gods and the Powers of mystification.

To the extent we are incapable and or unwilling to examine our lives as a function of human purpose and in doing so elucidate the True nature of our motives in relation to *equal* Goodness within our co-construction of reality, the entirety of human evolution and destiny is predominantly driven by our manifest will to Power *over*, i.e., our individual will to dominance, in *pursuit of unsubjectivity*.

Give and Aquire Voice @ uncommonsensatheory.com

APPENDICES

Appendix I

SAT MODEL

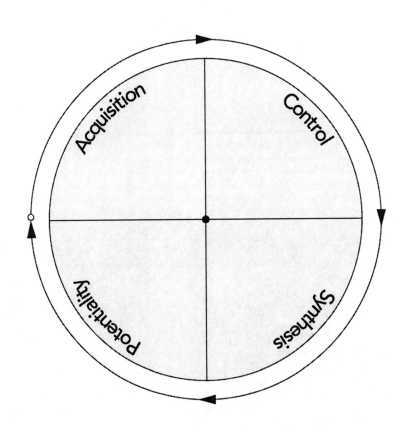

SAT MODEL

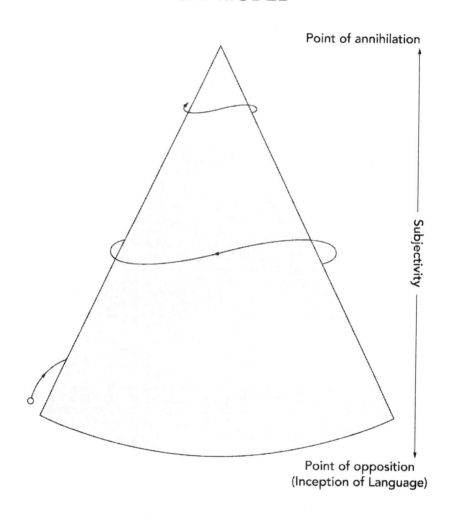

Point of annihilation

Subjectivity

Point of opposition
(Inception of Language)

PYRAMID OF POWER

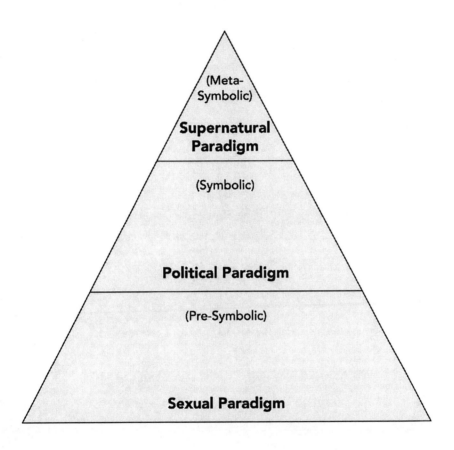

HIERARCHY OF MOTIVES

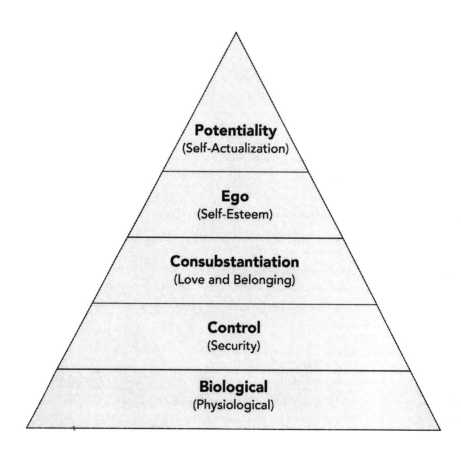

Potentiality
(Self-Actualization)

Ego
(Self-Esteem)

Consubstantiation
(Love and Belonging)

Control
(Security)

Biological
(Physiological)

TRUTH, POWER, & GOOD

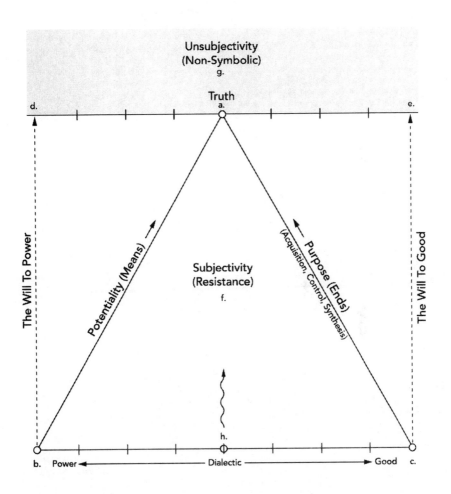

GLOSSARY

A posteriori
Reasoning or knowledge which precedes from observation or experience.

A priori
Reasoning or knowledge which precedes from theoretical deduction rather than from observation and experience.

Acquisition
The beginning phase of action in pursuit of unsubjectivity. A thing must first be acquired in order to have *potential* value.

Action-Routines
James A. Anderson & Elaine E. Englehardt's concept of: "semiotically encoded and recognizable performances. Action routines make sensible the acts which compose them. Acts are under the governance of the overarching understanding that allows them to be recognized as a component of a routine. the action routine is the sign of what's being done. It carries rules of performance and implicates the character of the enactor within those rules. The enactor is necessarily an agent of the routine."

Actus/Status
A Burkeian concept relating to the idea of status as *potentiality*, and actus as *actualization* wherein *action* requires passion and knowledge, and *status* requires resources. An Individual becomes what s/he is able to become according to a particular status (state), wherein becoming is dependent upon actus (action), which potentially augments or diminishes status.

Agenda-Setting Theory
An idea first elucidated by Maxwell McCombs and Donald Shaw, that the mass media does not tell you *what* to think, but rather tells you what to think *about*, i.e., by selecting (circumscribing) and filtering content, the consumer is "guided" towards what's "important."

Astro-theology
"Worship of the heavens" as practiced by ancient Egyptians. The basis of Western theological master narratives.

Axiom
A statement or proposition which is regarded as being established, accepted, or self-evidently true.

Beneficiary
The person or persons which have vested present or future beneficial interest in a trust. The holders of "equitable title" of trust assets as established by the grantor.

Big Bang Theory
The theory that the Universe began as a singularity which has expanded over 13.8 billion years. Inversely analogous to *Subjective Annihilation Theory* where the eventual annihilation of subjectivity represents a future "singularity" of human purpose.

Butterfly Effect
The idea that in a dynamic system, a small variance in conditions may over time become magnified and chaotic. This concept is analogous to everything we think, do, and say, within Symbolic Interaction.

Circumscribe
A Burkeian term used in reference to the manner in which we - through subjective language - call call forth particular aspects of "reality."

Citizen
A *beneficiary* of the state who, in applying for "benefits," exchanges Individual sovereignty for voluntary servitude, and therefore forfeits Individual rights in favor of "privileges" granted by the state.

Color of Law
The appearance of an act being performed based upon legal right or enforcement of a statute, when in reality no such (Lawful) right exists. Any statute or (legal) agreement disguised as a *Lawful* - and therefore binding - contract.

Color of Money
A purely symbolic form of money *as* value which is not backed by substance or anything of intrinsic value. See: **Money: Fiat**

Common-Sense
The conventional, the taken-for-granted, the quotidian, the assumed, etc. "common" sense is to inertia what uncommon sense is to energy.

Consubstantiation
Kenneth Burke's idea that, "in being identified with B, A is "substantially one" with a person other than himself. Yet at the same time he remains unique, an individual locus of motives. Thus he is both joined and separate, at once a distinct substance and consubstantial with another."

Control
The phase in pursuit of unsubjectivity wherein things of value must be managed in an organized, productive, and secure environment as a prerequisite to synthesis.

Creationism
The theoretical origin of existence according to the idea that reality must *necessarily* implicate a purposeful "creator."

Critical
From an uncommon sense perspective, the term "critical" is related to the term "discerning." According to Kenneth Burke, "*all animals are critics.*" To be critical is to be cautious and interested in a meaningful world. Many things in nature and society appeal to our instincts and lowest common denominators. To be critical is to evaluate meaning within the broadest of contexts.

Democracy
That form of government in which the sovereign powers reside in and are exercised by the whole body of free citizens directly or indirectly through a system of representation, as distinguished from a monarchy, aristocracy, or oligarchy. In a pure democracy the minority only has those privileges which are granted by the dictatorship of the majority. Socrates was executed by a democracy.

Dionysian/Apollonian
A concept develop largely by Friedrich Nietzsche that there is a perpetual struggle within the dichotomy of ideals. Dionysian being the paradigm of drunkenness, and the Apollonian the paradigm of reason. The dichotomy is also analogous to traditional gender roles.

Dishonor
In a lawful sense, to be in poor standing in relation to a contract or agreement, i.e., to *be* in violation or in default.

Dramatistic Pentad
Kenneth Burke's concept that communication is less about the exchange of ideas and more like a drama or play in which we act out scenes according to various combinations of motives, each originating within one or more combinations of "Act," "Scene," "Agent,"

Agency," and "Purpose." According to Burke: "*If action, then drama; if drama then conflict; if conflict, then victimage.*"

Esoteric
A mode of communication intended for or likely to be understood by only a small number of people sharing a specialized knowledge or interest.

Exoteric
A mode of communication intended for or likely to be understood by the general public.

Egocentric
Thought or action which is based upon a Power *over,* or Power *apart from* relationship with others.

Entropic Homeostasis
A state of gradual sustained decline.

Evil
That which is *perceived* as harmful or negative in relation to the *Individual.*

Evolution
The theoretical origin of existence according to the idea that everything observable changes over time, and that life tends to become increasingly complex over time.

Feminism
The advocacy of Women's rights on the grounds of political, economic, and social equality to men.

Form
In relation to value: beliefs, ideas, proposals, written procedures, rhetoric, hollow signifiers, e.g., fiat monies have little intrinsic value, rather their value relies upon *belief.*

Functions
The intended or unintended consequences of actions.

Manifest
The dominant motive or intention of an act.

Latent
The unintended consequence or "ulterior motive" of a manifest act.

GAAP
Generally Accepted Accounting Practices.

Gender
Socially constructed roles and behaviors specific to one's assumed biological sexuality.

Generalized Other
George Herbert Mead's philosophy that we develop a sense of self through social interaction. We do this as children through role play and later through the game stage wherein we learn not only our own expected roles, but also the expected roles of others and the rules by which they are enacted.

Genotype
The genetic constitution of an individual organism, i.e., the actual genetic makeup responsible for specific genetic traits.

God/Devil Terms
Terms, according to Richard M Weaver, which have "inherent potency" in identifying what is deemed politically correct/incorrect within a discursive community, e.g., "freedom," "Liberty," "Progress," as "God terms", and "Liberal," or "Conservative," or "Terrorist," as "Devil terms" according to assumed shared values.

Good
That which is *perceived* as beneficial or positive in relation to the Individual.

Guilt-Redemption Cycle

Kenneth Burke's idea that the effect of rejection within a hierarchy is guilt. All social conditions are hierarchical and complex with multiple potential expectancies placed upon Individuals. Participation within multiple social institutions creates inevitable conflict between expectations. In order to purge guilt the Individual must purify him or herself, either through "mortification" (self-sacrifice) or through "victimage," i.e., becoming the "scapegoat." Redemption is achieved in as much as the self-sacrificing or scapegoating achieves a redemptive level of purification.

Grantor

The person or entity which is responsible for the creation of a trust, typically by executing a trust agreement which details the terms and conditions thereof.

Hollow Signifier

In semiotics any symbol which can signify some other referent of meaning but who's meaning changes according to interpretation and context, e.g., the word "gay" may no longer mean, "lighthearted and carefree."

Hierarchy of Motives

Our Hierarchy of Motives is modeled after Abraham Maslow's theory of (Individual) needs, and likewise utilizes a pyramidal model as analogous to a hierarchy of motives. On a macro-social level *motives* are broader and more significant in relation to symbolic action in pursuit of human purpose.

Biological

Motives which originate in the physical evolution of humans, i.e., homeostasis, food, water, and sex, and are analogous to Maslow's Physiological "needs."

Control
Is implicated in all human motive as a process *of* empowerment. Anything of value must first be acquired and then somehow *controlled* in order that it may be synthesized into greater potentiality or Power. Control is analogous to Maslow's "safety," as in personal security, economic security, and health and well being.

Consubstantiation
The concept of persuasion, in as much as all human interaction is the process of persuading others to become similarly vested in one's particular values. This is analogous to Maslow's needs of, "friendship," "intimacy," and "family."

Ego
The thinking and feeling *Individual* will which is the central origin of motive. This is analogous to Maslow's "self-esteem," and "self-respect."

Potentiality
Power in pursuit of the greatest possible Power and is analogous to Maslow's "self-actualization," and self-transcendence."

Honor
In a lawful sense, to be in good standing in relation to a contract or agreement, i.e., to *not* be in violation or in default.

Human Action
A function of motive. Exclusive of autonomic functions of the body, i.e., heart beat, breathing, brain functioning, etc., all human activity is driven by *motive*, where human action is a manifestation of motive.

Hypothalamus
A small primitive part of the brain which regulates homeostasis in the body and is essentially common to all higher animal species.

Hierarchy of Needs
Abraham Maslow's human psychology theory suggesting that basic individual needs must be satisfied in order to progress upwards in a hierarchy of being, e.g., "physiological," "Safety," "Love and Belonging," "Esteem," and "Self-Actualization/"Self-Transcendence."

Law
Codified folkways, mores, and procedures.

Natural
A philosophy of law that is ostensibly determined by nature and therefore is universal.

Commercial
The body of law which applies to the rights, relations, and conduct of persons and businesses engaged in merchandising, trade, and sales, both Private and public.

Common
The ancient English law based upon societal customs and case precedents as opposed statutory law.

Statutory
Written laws typically enacted by a legislative body.

Political
An established legal practice area encompassing the intersection of politics and law.

Admiralty/Equity
An ancient form of military law with jurisdiction over International waters governing issues of criminal, civil, and International law.

Magna Carta
The first "great charter" of liberties forced from King John by the English barons at Runnymede, June 15, 1215, ensuring certain rights and liberties independent of the Crown.

Marginalized Individuals

Anyone who is not a member of a dominant class of Individuals due to: sex, gender, race, social class, ideology, etc.

Master Narratives

The dominant stories or fables which inform and unify a discursive community's values which become codified within it's laws, i.e., religious narratives of creation, transgression, redemption, etc.

Modern Money Mechanics

A book by the Federal Reserve Bank of Chicago describing the fractional reserve banking system and how money is created.

Money

An agreed upon medium for the efficient exchange of goods and services.

of Account

A manner of expressing value, as a benchmark by which to measure the relative value of goods and services.

of Exchange

A currency of any asset used to buy or sell good or services. Currency which is accumulated either physically or in a bank account, represent money as a store of value.

Occam's Razor

William of Ockham's maxim: When two competing theories have equal valence, the simpler one is the better.

Outside the Sphere

This phrase we use to expand upon the concept of unconventional or "uncommon" wisdom or sense-making which is more commonly referred to as thinking "outside the box." We use the term "sphere" as it is more applicable to subjective and abstract subject matter such as meaning and perception, as in the "*sphere of influence.*" Additionally, a sphere implicates a central point of significance which diminishes progressively as we move away from it's center. Spheres may also be perceived as multiple and overlapping depending on their contextual centers and or referential subject matter.

Outsider-Within
The concept from Standpoint Theory which supports the concept of observing social inequalities from the standpoint of marginalized Individuals. Those who are more subject to inequalities are more acutely aware of the nuances of injustice.

Phenomenological
A method of inquire based upon the premise that reality consists of objects and events as they are perceived or understood in human consciousness and not of anything independent thereof.

Phenotype
The outward manifest physical structure of a particular organism as an overall manifestation of it's overall genotypical traits.

Plato's Cave
Plato's Analogy of the Cave relates to the idea that we are all culturally conditioned to believe as we do. How we come to understand and view our world is inculcated from early on such that the ego becomes vested within a particular world view regardless of Truth.

Political Paradigm
The symbolic paradigm of Power which is based upon control of meaning in relation to human interaction.

Pollution
Kenneth Burke's term for the secular equivalent of Original Sin; an offense that cannot be avoided, or a condition that all people share.

Pyramid of Power
Our conceptual model of Power in the form of a pyramid representing three general paradigms of Power: the Sexual, the Political, and

the Supernatural. Power is organized therein according to to evolution of Power over time as well as hierarchy, beginning at the base and extending to the peak.

Potentiality
The phase in pursuit of unsubjectivity wherein things of value which have been synthesized into a new and greater forms become useful in pursuit of still greater resources, i.e., Power.

Power
The ability to do something.

With
Whatever "work" is being done is *equally* under the control, influence, and authority of those of whom are implicated and therefore vested in it's benefits.

Over
The ability to do *otherwise*; were there a conflict of interest between two or more competing groups or Individuals, the group or Individual with greatest power could exercise it's will regardless of the will of the other.

Apart from
Power which is neither controlled, influenced, nor under the authority of another, nor has control, influence, or authority over another.

Purification
Kenneth Burke's term for the cleansing needed to rid ourselves of language-caused guilt in order to achieve redemption.

Quantum Theory
Quantum mechanics is concerned with physical properties of matter on the *micro*, as opposed to the *macro* level of observation, i.e., the smallest quantum's of matter and energy and their associated behaviors. Quantum Theory is analogous to uncommon-sense making in that it requires a "quantum leap" in sense-making and suggests that

we are merely at the beginning in our search for Truth and human purpose.

Reality
A social construction based in *belief* as a result of Symbolic Interaction. There *may* in fact be fantastic intelligent civilizations terraforming worlds in some distant region of the Universe, however, no matter how probable or likely, the only way we can come to "know" of them is *through* language. Once a "thing" has been "real"-ized, it can always be made ever *more* "real" through language, e.g., mathematics, new technologies, increasing knowledge, etc.

Relativity: Special and General
Special Relativity is in reference to the constant speed of light (186,000 miles per second) for all observers regardless of speed or direction of motion. *General Relativity* essentially describes the distortion of the time-space continuum by massive objects. *Special Relativity* is somewhat analogous to the "constant" of *Subjective Annihilation Theory*, as *Special Relativity* is somewhat analogous to "gravities of "Truth" and meaning and their influence upon human interaction.

Republic
That form of government in which the powers of sovereignty are vested in the *people* and are exercised by the *people*, either directly, or through representatives chosen by the *people*, to whom those powers are specially delegated, i.e., the sovereign individual is free to reject the majority group-think.

Resistance
The force in opposition to Power, i.e., in nature, physical inertia. Within Symbolic Interaction, the willful opposition to any position of Power, most commonly in opposition to Power *over*.

SAT Model
Our conical model which depicts our evolution *towards* unsubjectivity. The base representing our subjectivity in nature, and the peak representing it's eventual annihilation through symbolic action.

Sapir-Whorf Hypothesis
A hypothesis holding that the structure of a language affects the perceptions of reality of it's speakers and thus influences their thought patterns and world views.

Semiotics
The study of signs and symbols and their use and interpretation. Everything is a sign but not everything is a symbol.

Sex
The anatomic distinctions of an individual's reproductive and secondary sexual characteristics based in biology.

Sexual Paradigm
The pre-symbolic human biological paradigm of Power based upon *successful* sexual reproduction.

Spiral of Silence
Elisabeth Noelle-Neumann's Theory that Individuals are fearful of isolation from the dominant social group and therefore tend to refrain from giving voice to ideas and beliefs which are perceived to be in opposition to popular opinion. Media plays a significant role in Individual's perception of the dominant ideology as well as what said ideology may entail. However, one's assessment of the social environment may not always correlate with reality.

Standpoint Theory
Sandra Harding and Julia T Wood's *Standpoint Theory* suggests that "through strong objectivity and the outsider-within phenomenon, marginalized individuals are placed in a unique position to point to patterns of behavior that those immersed in the dominant group culture are unable to recognize."

Subjective Annihilation Theory (SAT)
All things are subject to other things and conditions. Humans respond to subjectivity by seeking to continually reduce and eliminate it. Ultimately, there is no limit to this natural drive other than complete annihilation. Hence, subjectivity is the basis of human motive, and therefor action in pursuit of it's eventual annihilation.

Subjectivity
A state of being relating to, or characteristic of, one who is a *subject*. Especially, in lack of freedom of action, or in submissiveness.

Substance
Commodities, assets, means of production, tangible goods, e.g., gold has historically been recognized as having tangible value.

Supernatural Paradigm
The meta-symbolic Paradigm of Power based upon control of the meaning *of* meaning in relation to ultimate human purpose.

Symbol Using/Abusing Animal
The Burkeian concept that humans are unique in that we use symbols to rise above nature, but we also use them to pollute and destroy ourselves.

Symbolic Evolution
Human evolution as a consequence of the rise of the symbolic, i.e., all technological evolution post pre-symbolic evolution, particularly the evolution of the *meaning* of meaning.

Symbolic Interaction
A sociological concept which explains social behavior in terms of how people interact with each other through the use of symbols, i.e., words, gestures, and other symbols which have acquired conventionalized meaning.

Symbolic Representation
Any abstract symbol which *re*-presents another thing or idea such as written and spoken language, is symbolic representation. Essentially, all communication is symbolic in as much as even mimicked meanings such as the word "quack" or pointing in a direction are understood *within* a larger context of symbolic meanings.

Synthesis
The phase in pursuit of *unsubjectivity* wherein things of value, which have been controlled, become greater than the sum of their parts and useful as greater potential in the acquisition of still greater power.

Technology
In the broadest sense, specialized knowledge or knowledge of technique. Any form of knowledge implies a potential *lack of* knowledge. In a far as knowledge is Power, technology *is* Power *over* ignorance.

Terministic Screens
Kenneth Burke's idea that symbols become a sort of screen or grid of intelligibility through which we make sense of the world. Words, how we use them, and how we are culturally conditioned by them, necessarily reflect *some* viewpoints while deflecting *others*, i.e., there is no "neutral" nor "objective" meaning.

Trustee
The person, or persons appointed to impartially manage all duties required of a trust. Typically that acting trustee is named specifically within the trust instrument.

Truth
A shared *belief* held in common within a particular discursive community.

UCC
Universal Commercial Code.

Uncertainty Reduction Theory
Uncertainty creates cognitive dissonance which Individuals attempt to reduce between them. Reduction of uncertainty begins through information seeking and questioning. Information obtained can be instrumental in forming or avoiding relationships. The process of information seeking follows predictable stages: Verbal output, non-verbal warmth, information seeking, self-disclosure, reciprocity, similarity, and liking.

Essentially all communication is a form of uncertainty reduction.

Uncommon-Sense
The opposite of "common sense," e.g., the conventional, the taken-for-granted, the quotidian, the assumed, etc. *Uncommon Sense* is related to Albert Einstein's idea that - "*the problems of this world cannot be solved at the same level of thinking which got us into them.*" However for our purposes the term does not merely relate to "problem" solving, but rather to the deepest well of meaning from which "problems" *and* "solutions" arise.

US Bill of Rights
An addendum to the US Constitution intended to assuage concerns of the Anti-Federalists, guaranteeing a number of Individual freedoms, limiting the powers of government, and reserving some powers to the states and the public.

US Constitution
A contract which constitutes the debt of *The People* to the International financiers, thereby creating surety through the exchanging of the *sovereign* United States of *America*, for the *corporate*, for profit, United States.

Voice
Giving expression to a particular world view according to Individual standpoint through symbolic interaction.

REFERENCES

Adams, Samuel. *"such a Professional army"*

Anderson, James, A. and Engelhard, Elaine, E. *The Organizational Self & Ethical Conduct: Sunlit Virtue & Shadowed Resistance.*

Black's Law Dictionary.

Baum, L. Frank. *The Wizard of OZ.*

Berger, Charles, and Calabrese, Richard. *Uncertainty Reduction Theory.*

Burke, Kenneth. *A Grammar of Motives; Dramatistic Pentad.*

CFR. *Sec. V.*

Durkheim, Emile. *"Suicide."*

Debord, Guy. *Society of the Spectacle.*

Einstein, Albert. *Special and General Relativity, Big Bang Theory.*

Federal Reserve Bank of Chicago. *Modern Money Mechanics.*

Franklin, Benjamin. *US Constitutional Convention 1787.*

Geertz, Clifford. *Politics, Ritual, Power.*

Griffin, G. Edward. *The Creature from Jekyll Island.*

Harding, Sandra, and Wood, Julia, T. *Standpoint Theory.*

Jaikaran, Jacques, S. *Debt Virus.*

Madison, James. *"the means of defense."*

Maslow, Abraham. *The Hierarchy of Needs.*

McCombs, Maxwell, and Shaw, Donald. *Agenda-Setting Theory.*

Mead, George Herbert. *The Generalized Other.*

Nell. The Movie.

Nietzsche, Friedrich. *The Will to Power, "The Opiate of the Masses."*

Noelle-Neuwmann, Elizabeth. *The Spiral of Silence.*
Plato, *Analogy of the Cave, Theory of Forms.*
Richards, I.A. *Sapir-Whorf Hypothesis.*
Shakespeare, William. *"All the World's a Stage."*
Socrates, *"The Nature of Evil."*
The Federalist Papers.
Thoreau, Henry David. *"The unexamined Life."*
Wachowski, Andy, and Larry. *The Matrix.*
Weaver, Richard M. *Ethics of Rhetoric.*
Weber, Max. *"Fish Suspended in Water."*

INDEX

ABOUT THE AUTHOR

JR Miller is an independent-minded student of life, a renaissance man, and a connoisseur of socially critical expression in pursuit of the Good.

9 781683 481416